OPTIMIST RACING

Second Edition

" Phil Slater was my first racing coach, and his wife Jill taught me to sail.
I used the techniques in this book to help me win the Oppie Nationals,
and compete in four Oppie Worlds. Later, I used many of the same
techniques to win the Laser Nationals, Europeans, Worlds and Olympics.
I am sure they will help you too.
See you out on the water! "

Ben Ainslie

Olympic Gold Medallist 2000
Olympic Silver Medallist 1996
Olympic Gold Medallist 2004

www.fernhurstbooks.co.uk

OPTIMIST RACING

Phil Slater

First published in 2001 by Fernhurst Books, Duke's Path, High Street, Arundel BN18 9AJ
Tel 01903 882277, Fax 01903 882715,
Email sales@fernhurstbooks.co.uk, Website www.fernhurstbooks.co.uk

First edition published 1995

Printed and bound in China through World Print

British Library Cataloguing in Publication Data:
A catalogue record for this book is available from the British Library.

ISBN 1 898660 87 5

Acknowledgments
Phil Slater would like to thank the following UK team and Restronguet Sailing Club members
for sailing past his camera: James Austin GBR3938, Nicky Muller GBR3939, Pippa Welfare GBR4108,
Andrew Walsh GBR3913, Josie Gibson GBR4119, Adam Davis GBR3930, Libby Greenhalgh GBR4112,
Phil Dobson GBR3806, Leigh McMillan GBR4163, Amelia Goode GBR3847, Tim Boone GBR4197,
Nicola Barnes GBR4199, Paul Campbell-Jones GBR3534.
Thanks also to Sophie Hulbert for modelling the fitness exercises, those pictures being taken by
Philip Mitchell. I must thank Roddie Ainslie and Jim Saltonstall for encouraging me to start writing,
and Cathy Foster and Eddie Shelton for their support and advice. My greatest thanks must go to
my wife Jillian for her support and to Matthew and Verity, our children, who inspired my interest
in Optimist racing and coaching. I dedicate this book to the Optimist Class in which I and my family
have had many years of fun and friendship.
I must thank Lewis Dann and Robin Staite for their helpful suggestions on updating the first edition, Robert
Wilkes for the IODA statistics and Eddie Shelton for his thoughts on speed and downwind sailing.

Photographic credits
Cover photos by Peter Bentley. All other photos by Phil Slater
except fitness exercise photos by Philip Mitchell.

Edited by Jeremy Evans
DTP by Creative Byte, Poole
Cover design by Simon Balley
Text set in 10pt Rockwell Light

Contents

INTRODUCTION

Many people look on the Optimist as a bit of a joke. It's a curvy box that kids learn to sail in! Not so many people are aware that it is numerically the biggest sailing class in the world, and that ex-Optimist sailors won gold medals in all the dinghy classes at the Barcelona Olympics. The boat is, in fact, a remarkable design - an easily-controlled thoroughbred racing dinghy that provides superb one-design racing, and responds to and rewards the highest skills of top sailors.

The Optimist is sailed by over 170,000 young people in over 90 countries. Fantastic events take place all around the world, with racing of the highest standard and great fun ashore. Each year there are open meetings, national championships, area championships and a World Championship for as many as 250 sailors from 59 countries.

International Optimist racing is an adventure! It offers the chance of making lasting friendships with top sailors from other countries, and representing your country in major international competitions. This book will get you into the action. Its aims are:

- To help competent Optimist sailors develop handling techniques and boatspeed. They should be able to analyse performance, coach themselves, and develop a positive psychological attitude to the stresses of competition to get to the top in national and international racing.
- To help parents analyse their own motives for supporting their children's sailing, and to avoid actions that might have a negative effect on their performance and happiness.
- To help coaches develop competitor/ parent/coach relationships, to understand the constraints of children's development, and to develop race training programmes and techniques.

Performance depends on physical fitness, mental fitness, boatspeed techniques, boat handling skills, theoretical knowledge, ISAF rules knowledge, racing experience, good equipment, parental support and good coaching. Read on to find out how to achieve all these goals.

Part One
SPEED

1 SPEED BASICS

Sailing fast is the aim of all top sailors! It's great to leave the starting line and feel the boat drawing ahead, looking back and knowing you have the speed and the other boats are not going to catch you. But how do you gain such speed?

Some people seem to sail fast naturally, while others never get a top ten result. The single thing that will help you go faster is to **spend as much time as possible sailing.** Get to know the feel of your boat - how she responds to changes of wind strength and wave state. You will begin to feel when the boat is balanced, when she sails herself with only small movements of the tiller. You will recognise how the balance is changed by trim, mast and daggerboard rake, sail sheeting and, upwind, the relative value of sailing fast and free or pointing high but footing slower.

Learn the skills of sailing upwind and down in light, medium and heavy weather, in smooth and rough water, on lakes and the open sea. Learn to sit at the boat's pivot point, leaning back, balanced, allowing your upper body to float freely as the boat moves easily through the waves. Learn efficient boat handling, power hiking and bailing. Seek to gain automatic reflex boat control. Allow – trust your body to do the sailing while you keep your mind busy monitoring sail trim, tactics, tides, stress etc.. Learn to sail in a state of relaxed concentration, get 'in the groove', 'slip into the fast lane'…..!

Speed! Feel it, live it and spot anything that might damage it.

BALANCE

A boat is in balance when it virtually sails itself with the rudder pointing along the centreline, producing minimal drag. A balanced boat is a fast boat; always seek balance.

- Weather helm is present when the tiller needs to be pulled to windward to keep the boat sailing in a straight line.

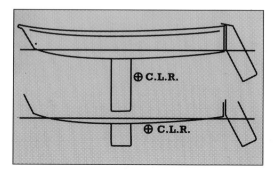

The CLR moves back when the board is lifted.

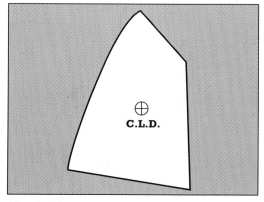

The CLD is positioned about here.

Weather helm.

Balanced helm.

● Lee helm is present when the tiller needs to be pushed to leeward to keep the boat sailing in a straight line.
● If the rudder is needed to keep the boat on course it is slowing you down.

CLR versus CLD The Centre of Lateral Resistance (CLR) is the point under the boat where the combined force of water pressure on the hull and foils (daggerboard and rudder) resisting sideslip or 'leeway' is centred. The Centre of Lateral Drive is the point in the sail where all the sideways forces are centred. If the CLD is aligned with the CLR, the boat is balanced. If the CLD is forward of the CLR, the boat's bow will bear off from the wind. This gives 'lee helm'. If the CLD is behind the CLR, the boat's bow will turn up into the wind. This gives 'weather helm'.

Mast rake Rake is important in the search for a balanced boat. If the mast is raked back, the sail's CLD acts behind the CLR,and turns the boat into the wind. If the mast is raked forward, the sail's CLD acts forward of the CLR, making the boat bear away.

Daggerboard angle & height When the daggerboard is fully down you can use the elastic loop (attached to the sides of the case) to hold it vertical, raked forward, or raked aft. When the daggerboard is raked forward, the CLR moves forward. When the board is raked back, the CLR moves back. If the boat was in a state of balance with the daggerboard vertical, raking it forward would give you weather helm and raking it back would give you lee helm.

In heavy weather you may need to lift the daggerboard to decrease the heeling moment and cut down weather helm. As the underwater portion of the daggerboard decreases, the CLR moves up and back towards the rudder. To keep the boat in balance, the mast can be raked back as the daggerboard is lifted. Lightweights will heel in heavy weather, so keep balance by lifting the daggerboard with the mast upright or forward.

Sheeting the sail As the sail is sheeted in towards the centreline the CLD moves back and makes the boat head up into the wind. This can be used to tack a stationary boat - you simply pull the boom across slowly, and the boat will spin through the wind. Similarly, balance changes when the sail is let out in gusts.

Sail shape Due to its cut or the way it is set, sail shape can considerably affect the balance of a boat. An over-tight leech moves the CLD back, while an open leech has the opposite effect. The sprit and vang (kicking strap) are important, because of their effects on the leech.

Below: Allowing the boat to heel will make it want to turn.

Heeling (Lateral trim) The asymmetric underwater shape, and in particular the effect of water pressure on the submerged lee bow, causes the boat to turn away from the immersed side. Heel can be used on all legs of the course to balance the boat and sail more quickly. For example, you can heel to windward on

If you sit too far back, the transom drags due to eddies and turbulence.

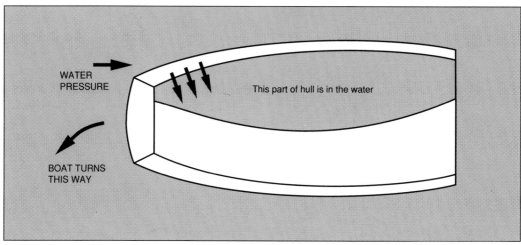

the beats to balance weather helm; on the run heeling to windward balances the rotational force of the mainsail; bearing away round marks is much easier if the boat is heeled to windward.

If you sit too far forward the bow transom hits the waves and stops you.

ESSENTIALS

- Hold the tiller extension like a dagger, little finger nearest the universal joint.
- Hold the mainsheet in the same way, little finger nearest the block.
- Hike leaning back, pulling the sheet with your elbow high.
- Keep the boat and rig balanced, and the rudder on the centreline.
- Don't let the bow hit waves. Bail, and sail to keep the boat dry.

Fore-and-aft trim The two aims in trimming the boat fore-and-aft are to try to prevent the bow transom from hitting the waves, and to try to prevent the stern transom dragging too deeply in the water. This is achieved with the boat sailing with its sheer line level. Lightweights will have to sit well back in moderate to fresh winds to prevent the bow from dipping. Heavyweights have to strike a happy medium, accepting some stern drag while keeping the boat dead flat which allows the bow to lift as high as possible.

STEERING WITHOUT THE RUDDER
Using the rudder always slows the boat down. You can steer the boat without the rudder, using the following techniques:

1 A boat with lee helm can be balanced, or a balanced boat may be made to luff (turn into the wind) by:
- Heeling to leeward.
- Bringing the CLD of the sail aft - by raking the mast back, sheeting in the sail more, or tightening the leech.
- Bringing the CLR forward - by raking the daggerboard forward.

2 A boat with weather helm can be balanced, or a balanced boat can be made to bear away (turn away from the wind) by:
- Heeling to windward.
- Bringing the CLD of the sail forward - by raking the mast forward, easing the sail, or opening the leech.
- Bringing the CLR aft - by raking the daggerboard aft or raising it.

3 Lash the tiller in the centre with elastic hooked around the toestraps; then practise the techniques above.

2 SAIL AND RIG

SAIL SHAPE

Sail shape is the key to pointing high and sailing fast.

Pointing depends on the sail's entry, which is the angle between the front of the sail and a line from luff to leech. If this angle is narrow (B) the entry is said to be flat and the boat will point high without backwinding. If wide, the entry is full (C) and the boat will point poorly. The point of maximum depth of a sail is called its 'belly'. The **power** or drive of a sail depends on the depth and the position of the belly. Generally:

- Full sails are more powerful than flat ones.
- A sail's power increases as the belly moves forward.
- A well-shaped sail has its belly $^3/_8$ to $^1/_2$ of the way back from the luff (A).

In sail setting you are seeking the best compromise between pointing and power.

In smooth water the boat is not being slowed by waves and can maintain maximum speed with less power. Thus pointing ability is most important, so set up with a flat entry, fullness further back and a flatter sail.

In rough water wave impact slows the boat and maximum power is needed to keep the speed up. Set up with the belly forward, a wide entry and a full sail.

The belly moves towards the relatively tighter side of the sail - forward if the luff is tightened, aft if the leech is tightened and down if the foot is tightened.

Sail Drive The drive from a sail is due to the pressure difference between the

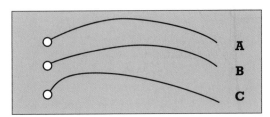

windward and leeward sides. The forces trying to push the boat sideways are cancelled by the force of the water on the daggerboard and rudder foils. With a properly trimmed sail all the forces are driving forwards.

Hooked Leech At no time should your coach, when following straight behind your boat, be able to see the leeward side of your sail. When the leech is hooked in towards the boat's centreline, the driving force from the leech works backwards which is not good!

A hooked leech is one of the commonest reasons for Opi sailors going slowly, but how does this come about?

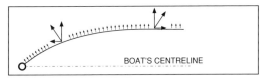

With a correctly trimmed sail (which has the leech parallel to the boat's centreline), the boat drives forward.

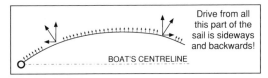

With an incorrectly trimmed sail that 'hooks' the leech inside the centreline, the driving force is sideways and backwards.

1 Excitement and over-sheeting.

2 Not knowing what a sail looks like when it is 'just right'.

3 Too much sprit tension - failure to readjust the sprit for falling wind strength, so the leech tightens and the boat stops in the lulls.

4 Variable wind strength - setting the sprit up for the gusts rather than the lulls.

5 Too much vang tension - none is required upwind in an Opi, except when spilling wind.

6 Foot of the sail too slack.

7 Luff too slack or badly laced.

It helps to mark a horizontal line on the leech between the battens. Keep this parallel to the boat's centreline when close hauled. If it angles towards the stern, the leech is hooked. Beware! Leech telltales do not always tell you the leech is hooked.

RIG CONTROLS

Sprit The key to understanding the sprit is to realise that the head of a sail cannot be stretched. Sprit thrust holds up the peak and tensions the the leech.

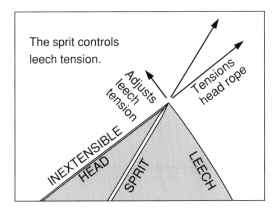

Clew Outhaul Besides flattening the foot, the clew outhaul moves the leech away from the mast, opening the leech and flattening the sail.

Top horizontal tie, tack horizontal tie, luff ties These alter the luff curve, which controls entry and fullness.

Top diagonal tie, tack diagonal tie (boom jaw uphaul) These control luff length (entry and sail shape), position the sail on the mast, and control luff tension. The top diagonal tie stops the throat of the sail moving up the mast when the sprit tackle is tightened. The tack diagonal tie controls the height of the boom. It is shortened by twisting it the required number of times before hooking it onto its pin.

Vang (Kicker/kicking strap) This holds the boom down offwind, tensions the luff and leech, and counters the vertical push of the sprit. If the sprit is tightened before the kicker, the top of the luff will form loose folds. In light weather when the luff is slack, virtually no kicker tension is needed. In medium weather the vang should be just slack when closehauled, but tight enough to control sail twist offwind. In heavy weather it must be tight to tension the luff and maintain leech tension when the sail is spilled.

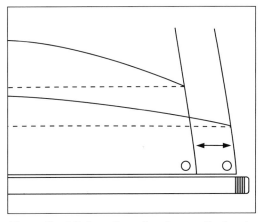

The outhaul flattens the sail and opens the leech.

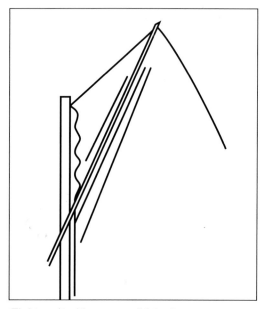

Tight sprit with no vang (kicker).

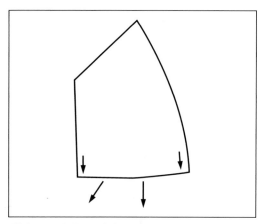

Kicker and sheet tighten the luff and leech.

SETTING UP THE RIG

1 Carefully tie the mast ties and the top and tack horizontal ties for the desired sail shape.
2 Set up the top diagonal tie. This tie cannot be adjusted without taking the mast down. To calibrate the rig the tie should be adjusted to keep the top of the sail at the same height. Do this by putting marks at the top of the sail luff and the top of the mast that line up when the top diagonal tie is the right length. The marks should be positioned so that when the luff is slack the sail measurement band is just below the top mast measurement band. When maximum luff tension is applied the sail measurement band will be just above the lower mast measurement band.
3 Put the mast up, and carefully tie the mast retaining loop.
4 Set up the sprit tackle just enough to take the slack out of the top diagonal tie.
5 Set up the desired luff tension by choosing how many twists to put into the tack diagonal tie (boom uphaul). Put a scale strip on the front of the mast to line up with the top of the boom jaws. Keep a record of the readings, so you can set your sail perfectly each time.
6 Apply the desired amount of vang tension. Tightening the sheet first makes this easier.
7 Apply the desired amount of sprit tension.
8 Finally, adjust the outhaul.

SAIL SHAPE FOR DIFFERENT WIND STRENGTHS

Every time you sail record your sail shape on a Race Training Analysis sheet (see page 95), along with your comments on wind and sea conditions and how the boat performed. This helps to build up confidence, judgement and boatspeed.

Light wind settings (Force 1-2/1-4 knots/0.3-1.6 metres per second)

Slowly moving air will break away from a full sail, so aim to get a flat sail shape to prevent stalling and optimise acceleration/pointing. Aim for the draft halfway back, with a slack luff and slack

RIG CONTROLS

1 Rudder
2 Tiller
3 Tiller extension
4 Daggerboard
5 Daggerboard case
  with elastic
6 Bulkhead
7 Bow transom
8 Side
9 Gunwale
10 Buoyancy bags
11 Mast thwart
12 Toestraps
13 Mainsheet
14 Top mainsheet
  block
15 Mainsheet span
16 Mast
17 Mast securing line
18 Sprit
19 Sprit tackle
20 Boom
21 Boom jaws
22 Vang
23 Sail tie
24 Eyelet
25 Cringle
26 Luff
27 Head
28 Leech
29 Foot
30 Peak
31 Throat
32 Tack
33 Clew
34 Outhaul
35 Foot or shelf seam
36 Batten
37 Leech telltale
38 Telltales
39 Burgee
40 Painter

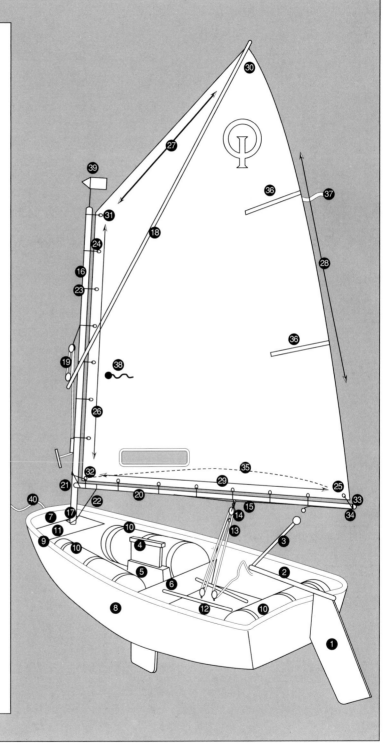

Use baseline marks on sail and masthead.

leech. You want a convex luff curve, flattening the belly and entry.

- Top horizontal tie/tack horizontal tie - Set at 9mm gaps.
- Centre luff tie - No gap, but other luff ties set to give an evenly curved luff.
- Luff tension slack - Put several twists in the loop of the tack diagonal tie, lifting the boom. With the luff slack the belly moves back, the entry flattens, and the leech tightens.
- Outhaul - Pull out to band, which re-opens leech and flattens sail.
- Vang - Totally slack.
- Sprit - Slacken until a small crease appears at the throat. This shows you are not over-spritted and the leech is open.
- Boom jaws - Must be tight on the mast, but must allow the boom to lift as leech

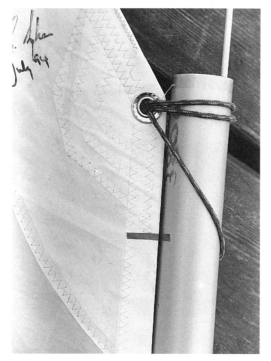

Adjust the top diagonal tie to keep these marks in line.

A boom level calibration scale allows you to record exact luff tension.

tension increases. To achieve this, file away the upper inside edge of the centre of the jaws. Low-friction deck sleeve and pin step are essential, or the mast will stick when you are tacking which will affect sprit tension and the set of your sail.

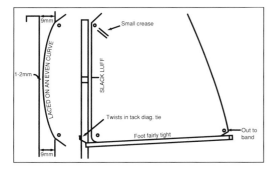

Gusty winds in all conditions

Always set up your rig, and particularly the sprit, for the lighter wind in the lulls. When a gust comes it will open the leech and you will be able to sail through it. A rig with correct sprit and leech tension for the gusts will have a tight hooked leech in the lulls - deadly!

Full power settings (Force 2-4+/4-11+ knots/1.6-5.5+ metres per second) Set the sail with a straight luff and loose foot.

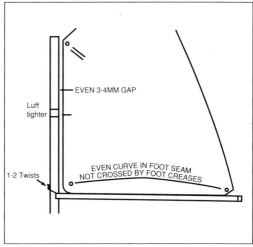

- Luff lacings, top and tack horizontal ties - Adjust them to give an even 3-4mm gap along the whole luff.
- Outhaul - Ease so the shelf seam is not crossed by the foot creases. If the foot is too slack the leech hooks.
- Vang - Just slack when the main is sheeted going upwind.
- Sprit - As for light winds with a small crease at the throat.
- Luff tension - Adjust by taking off enough twists from the tack diagonal tie to firm the luff. As the wind increases the luff must be tightened.

Left: Don't let the leech hook due to a lull in the wind. Adjust the sail shape for the lulls, and accept that the leech will open in the gusts.

Heavyweights

Heavy sailors can carry powered-up sails until racing is abandoned. The mast will bend, and to maintain the shape and power of the sail it is necessary to set up the top and tack horizontal ties tightly, and ease the central luff ties to give an even curve with a middle lacing gap of about 9mm.

HEAVY WEATHER: Bending mast depowers the sail

EVEN TIGHT LACINGS

TIGHT FULL LENGTH LUFF

Depowering

You need to take another look at the rig if you're hiking hard with the daggerboard raised 4in (10cm) and raked back, but are still spilling wind in the gusts and on wave tops, and are finding it difficult to keep the boat driving without heeling.

● Lace all luff ties with the eyelets hard up, touching the mast.
● Move the leech as far away from the mast as possible by tightening the outhaul to pull the clew to the black band. This flattens the lower half of the sail.
● Ease the top horizontal tie to give an 8mm gap. This flattens the upper half of the sail. Allow for stretch - maximum gap 10mm. Top ties must be very strong. They take all the sprit pull along the headrope as well as the sail's pull. They

do most of the mast bending, and if they break the sail can tear.
● Tack horizontal and vertical ties must be tight.
● Luff must be as tight as possible. Heavyweights depower with evenly-spaced luff lacings, as mast bend is flattening the entry for them.
● Vang is important upwind to maintain leech tension when the sail is spilt. Apply as much tension as possible.
● Sprit must be as tight as possible, except for lightweights depowering below Force 4 who will need to set the sail with the small throat crease.

To depower use a tight outhaul, tight sprit, tight luff and tight vang.

3 UPWIND SPEED

BAD HABITS

Take a look at top competitors in an international event sailing to windward. Most will be storming along, hiking hard and appearing to be going fast. Take a closer look. While some are sailing with a smooth continuous motion, others sail fast then pause, slowing before getting back to full speed, then slow again. Take a look at your own sailing. Do you sail smoothly and at maximum speed, or are you a pauser? It's easy to pick up bad habits which are hard to recognise and change.

- Do you luff too much in the gusts? Is this due to letting your boat heel too much? Should you be playing the mainsheet to keep her level?
- Are you fit enough to drive fast and hard for a whole beat? Are your hiking pants comfortable?
- Are your feet supported firmly by the toestraps in the right places? Do you wriggle from one leg to the other, and what happens to the boat when you do this?
- Do you really keep the boat level or heeled to windward? It's easy to get used to an angle of heel which is comfortable, but it may make the boat unbalanced. How about trying an inclinometer on your mast bulkhead to help change your style?
- Are you hitting waves with the bow or with your body?

PAIR OR 'BUDDY' TRAINING & TUNING

In the Optimist class top sailors have often had more than a lifetime's worth of suggestions hollered at them by well-meaning parents and coaches. It is much better to work out problems and other aspects of tuning and boatspeed for yourself, and the way to do this is by pair training.

Find a friend who is your size and about the same speed. Get into the habit of sailing together at every opportunity. Try different aspects of tuning, technique, daggerboard or mast rake, boat trim, and styles of hiking. Check out and criticise one another's sailing style and sail shapes, discussing settings for the day. If one of the boats is sailing like a drain, two heads are better than one to sort out the problems. Pair tuning gives you confidence - on the day of the big race, after sailing for five minutes with your buddy, you will know your boat is as fast as ever.

Pair training: sail together, upwind and down.

Similar techniques to pair training can be used after the start. If you do not feel your boat is moving as she should, sail parallel with another boat and go into pair training mode. Check everything, then change something. Faster? Yes! Now sail away!

Working together The standard procedure for pair training is to sail on the same tack as your buddy, with the boats' bows level and their hulls two to four lengths apart. In this way, neither boat will be blanketed or backwinded by the other, and wash will not be a problem. Sail like this until one boat draws ahead. Stop when the boat behind gets disturbed air or hits the wake. Cruise together and chat about it. Then try again, changing over the windward and leeward stations. If the same boat draws ahead, raft up and discuss why. If you can't work it out, get the slower boat sailing with the other skipper watching. If he can't spot the problem, change over with the slower helm watching the faster boat.

You can also work on boat handling with 'follow-my-leader' sessions, and try close covering team-race-style duels. Then having tested your speed and technique you can try luffing like never before. Does it work? If so, go for it!

GROUP TUNING

Used by a group (with or without a coach) to check speed, pointing, sail setting, tune and technique. After a gate start, the boats aim to get three lengths apart, closehauled on the same tack. After a while you will see that some boats are sailing higher and some faster. Stop, compare settings, discuss, adjust and try again – to get everyone sailing high and fast!

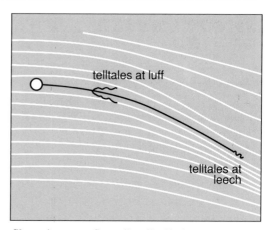

Slow air over a flat sail - all telltales are blowing back.

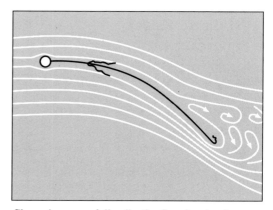

Slow air over a full sail - the flow has broken away from the back of the sail.

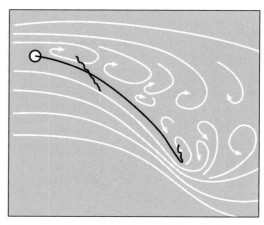

Slow air over an over-sheeted full sail - the sail is stalled with the flow totally broken away.

SMOOTH WATER UPWIND

Light wind Imagine the water like glass. The air is drifting very slowly across the sail. If the sail jerks, the air flow will break away and may take as long as one minute to adhere to the sail again. During that minute you have no drive! So you must sit absolutely still and concentrate on keeping the sail still and full, on the slightest twitch of the telltales, on the wind on your cheek, and on signs of the wind on the water. All movements must be in slow motion, whether your body, the sheet or the tiller. Tacking must be slow and smooth with maximum roll. The boat must be kept on its side until the sail is full and the bow is heading on or below the new course; the recovery roll must be slow and steady, with no jerks.

It may be necessary to heel the boat to leeward so the sail holds its shape and the boom does not fall towards the centreline. Find a comfortable position - perhaps sitting on the bottom of the boat with your feet down to leeward, or squatting in the centre with your weight on the leeward foot. Make sure you are far enough forward to keep the transom out of the water, or eddies will form behind and slow you down. Dipping the bow does not matter if there are no waves.

The sail must be set as flat as possible so that the slow moving air flows over it without breaking away. A full sail only has a fraction of the drive of a flat sail in drifting conditions since the air flow separates from the back half of the sail for much of the time, and total separation (stalling) occurs more easily. Set up as already mentioned with mast forward, luff slack, sail ties loose and the luff in a smooth convex curve; the leech must be slack, so set the sprit tension

loose enough to get a small crease at the throat. A thin, lightweight mainsheet makes sail handling easier, and sensitivity can be further improved by disconnecting from the bottom of the boom block to get a two-part purchase - a small, snap-hook is the neatest way to do this.

Remember to keep the boat moving at all costs. It is tactically more important to keep in the wind patches than to sail on lifts, so if your patch if fading head for the next. Don't be negative if you are heavy. Heavy sailors have won championship races in these conditions - in light airs the positive thinker wins!

Moderate wind The wind is strong enough to hold the boom to leeward, and the boat is trimmed with a slight heel to windward. The boat is so well balanced it sails straight with the tiller on the centreline. You sit forward by the bulkhead to keep the transom out of the water. In steady winds you could try sitting in to keep

windage down, but if the wind is variable or you are busy tactically it will pay to sit on the side. You may find that with the sail still flat you can sheet closer to the centreline and point higher than in any other conditions. Body movements, sheet adjustments, manoeuvres and tacks can be more robust. As the wind increases you can ease the outhaul to get maximum fullness and drive.

Before the race, get someone to check that your leech is not hooked. If your boat is slow the leech will almost certainly be the problem, so ease the sprit to get that small throat crease, check the vang is slack, take off a twist from the boom uphaul to tighten the luff a little, and if you are still slow pull out the outhaul by 1-2cm.

Light sailors can continue to sheet close and point high using flat sails in winds up to Force 3 on flat water. When small waves start forming and splashing up the bow it's time to sit further back and sail the waves!

SAILING IN WAVES UPWIND

Basic principles Many styles of wave sailing can be seen at international events. Different wave conditions pose different problems, but two basic principles always apply:

- It is vital that speed is maintained, and as little as possible of the boat's dynamic energy is lost negotiating each wave.
- Energy loss occurs when the boat and crew are slowed by pitching, by sailing uphill, and by wave impact on the bow transom, forward topsides or crew.

Pitching When a boat pitches, the ends move up and down. In waves the vertical movement of the ends speeds up, absorbing driving energy and slowing the boat down. The more easily the ends can lift, the less energy will be lost. This can be achieved by:

- Keeping the ends of the boat as light as possible. Food, drink, wet sponges, painters and paddles should all be stowed by the daggerboard box.
- Sitting at the point where the boat pivots, so the hull moves without moving your body. Only the boat pitches - you maintain your equilibrium and less energy is lost. At the Argentinian World Championships this was demonstrated most effectively by Ramon Oliden. He leant back, balancing on one leg on the point where the boat pivoted and sailed amazingly fast in the choppy conditions.

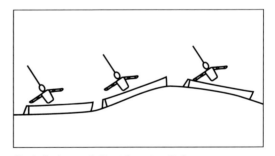

Body balanced: Boat free to pitch.

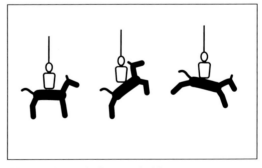

Rider balanced - horse pitching.

Uphill Energy and speed are lost when the boat has to rise to go over a wave. This is not a problem in chop, but gets troublesome as swell increases. Maintain speed at all costs or leeway will occur as the daggerboard stalls.

Power beating Hike the boat level as forcibly as you can, driving up and over the front face of each wave. Keep the power on, accelerating down the back of the wave until the short lull in the trough. Keep repeating this burst of power on every wave and you will be dramatically faster. Steer a weaving course, bearing away a little if threatened by a steep or breaking wave.

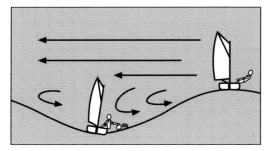

The natural lull in the trough can be used to heel to weather and scoop out a bailer of water.

Wave impact on the bow transom will kill boatspeed. The weather bow is particularly important because impact here results in water coming aboard.
● Sit back to lift the bow: sailors 45 kg or more sit 20 cm behind the bulkhead, smaller sailors sit up to 60 cm back in heavy weather.
● Heel the boat 5 degrees to lift the weather bow.
● Balance the boat by lifting the daggerboard.
● Sail fast and free.
● Allow the boat to pitch easily.

When bigger waves threaten to break against the bow, lean back momentarily to lift the bow over the crest. The boat will pause then accelerate as the waves pass. Sitting rigid will cause your body weight to be slowed down, so let your body move steadily and smoothly fore-and-aft at the waist and hips - whatever antics the boat gets up to! Wave impact on the crew can also seriously stop the boat. This is particularly likely if you hike with an 'S' style below the level of the gunwale. The answer is to watch the waves carefully, and straighten your legs and lift your body whenever a humpy one comes along.

Here the bow buries too easily in chop. The helmsman should lean back to lift the bow over each wave. As a general rule, sit further back when sailing in waves of all sizes.

Bailing: luff and heel to windward.

Lean in and take a scoop.

Chuck it out and bear off.

HEAVY WEATHER UPWIND

Common Problems

1 Poor bailing technique.

2 Excessive heel and inability to get bilge water to windward for bailing due to over-sheeting, slow spilling and poor hiking technique.

3 Uncontrollable luffing in gusts, and getting in 'irons'.

4 Capsizing - no real problem unless mast comes out of its step. If this happens, the mast will split the thwart when you right the boat. So check the mast-tie strings.

Why bail? Bailing is vital in heavy weather. If you can't keep your boat dry you will not survive the race! Fill a bucket with water and feel how heavy it is. Then pour it into your boat. It will spread out until it's hardly noticeable! If a few buckets of water are sloshing around they will make the boat heavy; she will not lift so well to waves; more water will break on board; and she will be harder to steer and keep upright. The weight of water to leeward counter-balances your hiking, the boat heels more, and weather helm gets extreme.

Bailing technique Do not stop the boat to bail. If the boat is kept sailing however slowly when you are bailing, you will not slip to leeward. Ease the main enough to get the boat heeling to windward, and keep your backside well out over the side. Lean in and scoop forward towards the bulkhead, or behind the bulkhead towards the windward topsides. Use the helm to keep the boat moving smoothly ahead and a little upwind, luffing if the sail threatens to heel the boat and bearing off if the main lifts or the boat slows too much.

Extend your body in the gusts.

Keep your body upright in the lulls.

Power bailing Now try sailing more sheeted, taking advantage of lulls in the wind or the troughs of the waves to lean in rapidly and scoop without losing any boatspeed. You will eventually find that with tiller and main in one hand, you can luff a little while hiking, and make the water cross the boat in a little wave. You can then lean in quickly and take a scoop as the water reaches the weather side, then lean out hard while bearing off, powering the boat up and over the next wave as you dump the water.

Hiking It pays to develop a straight-legged 'Laser' style, lifting your body off the water. Tall sailors have to do this anyway,

and straight-legged hiking has been shown to be less damaging to the knees.

Keep the boat driving at speed on the beat, hiking well out in a position you can comfortably keep up for the whole race. You then have a little bit of reserve power for short periods of extreme effort.

Gust sailing Keep the boat level by easing the sheet by straightening your arm at the elbow, and hiking hard and flat. As soon as you can sheet in again so you have some sheet to spill next time, and get back to your basic hiking position.

Do not luff in gusts when sailing on open water, or you will lose speed due to wave impact and decreased drive.

Daggerboard - Heavyweights

Heavier sailors can sail with the dagger-board fully down, but will benefit from raking it back if weather helm develops.

Daggerboard - Lightweights

Lighter sailors will need to lift the dagger-board progressively to decrease the heeling moment and help keep the boat level as the wind increases. Provided the boat is moving this will make virtually no difference to leeway, but will make the boat much easier to handle.

HEAVY WEATHER UPWIND SUMMARY

- The sail must be depowered. Set with tight luff, tight lacings, eased top tie, very tight sprit and vang.
- All except lightweights, keep the outhaul slack 1 cm to drive through the waves.
- Use cup mast step.
- Sit well back to lift the bow (see page 23).
- Heel 5 degrees to lift the weather bow.
- Hike hard and drive the boat. Spill wind in the gusts, don't luff.
- In lulls sheet in, lean in, bail when you can but keep moving.
- Sail free and fast. All except 'heavies' will go to windward with the boom end well outside the back corner of the boat.
- Maintain boat balance by lifting the daggerboard by up to 25 cm.
- Think before tacking. Look for a smooth-er patch, and tack on top of a wave. It can be a disaster if you tack into a curler.
- Getting stuck in 'irons' during a tack is a disaster. The boat stops and then starts blowing backwards. To get out of it, point the rudder in the direction you want the stern to go, and lift the daggerboard three-quarters of the way up. Pulling the boom to windward can cause unpredictable sheering.
- To get home in a 'hurricane', take down the sprit and sail in on the bottom half of the mainsail.

Sail free and fast with the boom end outside the boat unless you're a heavyweight.

4 DOWNWIND SPEED

SAIL TRIM

Downwind speed does not inevitably come by bearing off at the windward mark and easing the sail. It needs as much work and sensitivity to go downwind quickly as it takes up the beat. Off the wind the sail should continue to be trimmed on the luff and leech telltales, until the boat starts feeling dangerously unstable - as the boom moves forward of the mast, part of the sail's drive pushes the mast to windward. In light weather it is possible and desirable to sail downwind with the boom well forward of the mast. In this position, with the boat heeled to windward (kiting), gravity will hold the boom out. As the wind increases the lateral drive of the sail will help lightweights kite with more heel. With more wind, lightweights and then heavyweights will have to sheet in progressively to prevent a death roll to windward. In these conditions the vang needs to be increasingly tightened to

On the reach all telltales must blow back. Slight windward heel can improve balance.

minimise sail twist. For reaching the sail needs to be full. For running, when it becomes impossible to keep the telltales blowing back, the sail should be flattened.

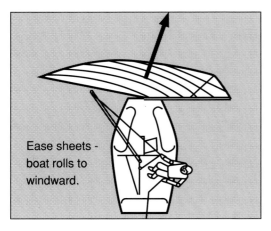

Ease sheets - boat rolls to windward.

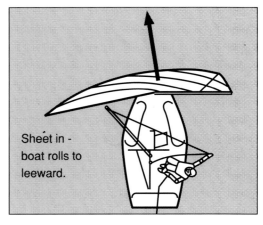

Sheet in - boat rolls to leeward.

DAGGERBOARD

It is common to see Ops going downwind with too much daggerboard.

Roll your boat and take a look at how much daggerboard projects with your favorite downwind settings. On the run the board should not project from the box at all, except in heavy weather. On reaches you only need enough board to prevent leeway.

Settings Try out different settings when doing speed exercises and pair training - you will be surprised how little dagger-board you need. For every centimetre your board is raised, you decrease surface area by 58sq cm, and reduce surface friction accordingly. Mark the back edge of the board at 4in (10cm) intervals for reference.

BOAT TRIM

Nosediving and drag Correct fore-and-aft trim is critical to reaching speed. If you are too far forward the bow transom digs in, kicking up a wave and increasing the wash. This can be risky for lightweights because it can lead to nosediving and broaching. If you are too far back, the water begins to bubble and eddy behind the transom. This is particularly damaging when you're sailing slowly. The water should slide away without a sign that the boat has passed. Heavyweights usually sink both the bow and stern transoms in light weather, and have to find a happy medium where drag is least. Lightweights can avoid bow and stern drag almost totally. Their problem is more one of getting back and out to keep the boat level with the bow lifting in the gusts.

KITING

Kiting is tricky, but is also the quickest way downwind in all wave states until planing becomes possible.

1. Centre of drive of the sail is over the centre of the boat, with one chine and most of the daggerboard lifted for minimal surface drag. The skipper holds the sheet above the ratchet block for least friction.

2. A jerk in on the sheet prevents the start of a windward roll.

3. Balance again means speed.

4. But it's followed by a death roll as the sail pushes the mast to starboard, the lee bow wash pushes the bow to port, and attempting to steer out of it aggravates the situation. The only solution is to lean in and jerk the sheet.

5. Back on an even keel, ready to kite again.

Beam reach/close reach In non-planing conditions, the boat should be heeled to weather to decrease wetted surface area and skin friction.

Broad reach/run On broader legs of the course, the boat tends to luff as the sail is eased because its drive becomes increasingly asymmetric. Balance this by heeling the rig to windward until the middle of the sail is over the hull. The effect of the immersed windward chine opposes the turning effect of the sail - a balanced boat with minimal wetted surface area means speed.

Technique You can use different methods to make the boat kite. Jam your aft foot under the straps, or plant it firmly under your body in the angle of the chine with your forward foot in the chine angle of the cockpit pointing forward. Experiment with different positions - I have seen an expert heavyweight sailor kiting and surfing with his front foot forward of the bulkhead. Some people rest a hand on the daggerboard, others grasp the toestraps. My feeling is that the forward hand should hold the mainsheet above the ratchet block, so the sheet can be played or pumped as necessary to maintain stability, drive and surfing. When trying to kite in waves take a straighter course, and use fore-and-aft trim and pumping to get maximum drive from the waves.

PLANING

It takes a fair breeze to get an Optimist up, but once they are away they really travel.

Technique In semi-planing conditions, get the boat dead flat and watch out for gusts. Sail a little high in the lulls. Just as a gust is about to strike, hike out (even if you heel a little to windward) and bear off with the gust. Give a pump (one per gust) and you are away! Keep the boat level at all costs by easing in the fiercest gusts, but immediately pull the sheet back in so you have something to spill next time. If you have spilt wind, but the boat is still on her ear, or if you are not strong enough to work the sheet, bear away as the gusts hit to keep the hull under the rig.

As the gust passes, luff to get to the next gust sooner and to maintain your course. Lightweights need to be able to hike on the back corner of the boat to stop the nose diving - arrange your toestraps to allow you to do this.

DOWNWIND WAVES

This is the pure essence of sailing! The pain of beating stops and pure magic happens. The aim is to keep sliding down the fronts or sailing the tops of the waves as long as possible. On the front face of a wave you have clear strong wind, can slide downhill, and have the water movement with you. That's your target area. Troughs are bad news because you lose the wind and the water movement slows you down.

Catching Waves So you're out on a perfectly honking day with a big swell rolling in. Taking a wave is like jumping onto a moving train. You've got to run fast before you jump, so head up and sheet in as your ride approaches and pump if you get a gust. (You're allowed one pump per wave and one pump per gust.) As the wave starts to lift the back of the boat, bear off hard down the wave, hike out and back, and watch out for the death roll. Feel the acceleration. The boat's got to get up to the speed of the wave or be left behind, so lean forward to dip the

1. The boat slows on the back of a wave.

2. The next wave comes up behind. Bear off, pump and lean back to prevent a nose dive.

3. Plane on the face of the wave.

4. Plane on the crest - the best ride of all!

Always keep your weight well back downwind in waves.

The aim is to keep sailing the tops of the waves or sliding down the fronts for as long as possible.

nose and increase sliding. Give a hearty pump, balanced by hiking out or back, and the boat will shoot forward again, accelerating to the wave's speed and slipping down the face of the wave. Note that if you shoot at Mach 3 straight down a steep face, you will overtake the wave, reach the trough, and possibly pitchpole. To prevent this, head up and sail along the wave.

To sail down the wave
- Bear away down the slope.
- Lean forward and then lean back before you dig in.
- Pump!

To sail up the wave
- Luff.
- Lean back more.
- Ease the sail.

Below left: Stay on the wave fronts!
Below right: Troughs are bad news.

Dropping off Sometimes you will slow down in the trough, having run out of wind and slope, and the wave will rush past and leave you behind. Alternatively, you may just miss the wave. The answer is to point up to keep your speed, sail high and fast along the back of the wave and in the trough, and finally bear off on the face of the next wave. In irregular waves it's necessary to watch their development like a hawk to grab a ride.

Pumping Lean in and grab the mainsheet, close to the rachet block or on the part leading from the boom to the rachet, and heave it as hard and fast and far as you can. To balance the boat you will have to lean out, and when the pump stops lean in again. You are only allowed one pump per wave, to initiate surfing or planing, and can move your body to trim the boat.

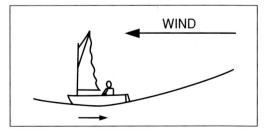

SAILING BY THE LEE

Over the last ten years sailors in classes with unstayed rigs have developed ability in sailing 'by the lee'. This helps downwind performance by giving:
- Freedom to manoeuvre, and more options on the run.
- Better chance of getting the inside position at the leeward mark.
- Starboard tack advantages for the whole run.
- The ability to bear off, away from covering boats.
- The ability to bear away to break overlaps.
- Freedom to ride wave faces in either direction.

The Racing Rules of Sailing define windward and leeward like this: When sailing by the lee or directly downwind, her leeward side is the side on which her mainsail lies. The other side is her windward side.

Begin to practise sailing by the lee in light winds and do not try to kite. Bear away, holding the extension at the UJ and crouching in the boat, leaning inboard. Let the sheet out progressively, keep bearing away until you are reaching along with the boom forward of the mast and the wind crossing the sail from leech to mast. Bearing away now makes the boat actually come up into the wind and eases the sail, while luffing fills the sail with wind, heeling the boat more.

Enjoy this for a bit, then try bearing away more until the bottom of the leech starts to flick: you are near to the gybing point. Either luff a little or ease the sheet to fill the sail. Fun! To get back to a normal run again, luff up slowly and pull in the mainsheet as you do it. Well done!

When racing you would not sail so high – keep the boom at 90 degrees to the centreline (less in strong winds).

In strong winds get your feet more into the middle, with the tiller extension on the leeward gunwale and your body leaning to leeward and facing forward. Everything works backwards! Ease the boat in the gusts by bearing away more and/or by pulling in the sheet. In the lulls power up by doing the opposite! In smooth water it's possible to kite by the lee.

Wave sailing by the lee gives you the ability to choose the fastest route downwind in waves - enabling you to stay on the wave face longer and helping you avoid the slow backs of the waves.

Here's an example. At the windward mark you are bearing away but a port tacker is coming. Give him more time to keep clear by going straight onto a run 'by the lee'. Rapidly ease the main until you heel to windward, move in and bear away sharply until the sail pressure eases. Now she's off! Straighten up! Wave! Pump! Planing on the face, wave travelling to left so ease and bear off. Surfing by the lee. Wave passing so luff up and try to keep up speed on its back. Here's another. Ease and bear off. Pump! Away again!

The result is a direct course in clear air, with a fast approach to the leeward mark where you take the inside turn!

Practise makes perfect! You must sail downwind in waves until your response to the characteristics of each wave becomes automatic, freeing you to ride them in the most effective manner.

Part Two
BOAT HANDLING & TACTICS

5 BASIC BOAT HANDLING

TACKING

The roll-tack Boatspeed may be maintained through a tack by roll-tacking. Here's how to do it.

1 When you decide to tack, bear away a little and heel the boat to leeward.

2 Then smoothly roll the boat right over to windward as you luff through the wind. By the time the hull is pointing on the new close-hauled course, the gunwale will be touching the water. Your feet should be under you, placed on the inside of the chine between the boat's bottom and side.

3 Stand up, bear off a little more so that the boat is just below the new close-hauled course, and place your foot across the boat to the inside of the windward chine.

4 Smoothly and carefully transfer your weight from one foot to the other, rolling the boat upright to her new beating trim.

5 Cross the boat and sit on the other gunwale. Do not let go of the tiller extension, but steer with your arm behind your back. Only when the boat is sailing well on the new tack should you change your hands round.

When practicing tacking, try counting yourself through the movements. Then try tacking as slowly as you can to the same count sequence. Next, try fast counting and tacking - you will find a particular rate of tacking will feel fast and comfortable. Keep practising until you tack perfectly without needing to count or even think about what you are doing. A lighter

1. Small wave - helm down!

2. Roll and duck.

sailor should ease the sheets slightly during a tack, and sheet in once the boat is balanced and driving on the new course. Don't tack on impulse. When a tack is needed keep driving, check for right of way boats, and look ahead for a flat patch. Tack on the top of a wave in one movement.

DOUBLE TACKING

Double tacking whilst stationary is an essential skill for Optimist sailors in the minutes before the start. While beating very slowly on starboard, tack onto port, sail for a boat length, and then tack back to starboard and stop. The entire double tack must be achieved as quickly as possible to avoid the risk of impeding a starboard tack boat. The initial tack from being stationary on starboard to port is achieved by rolling well to windward for acceleration, and then pulling the boom across to increase spin. The boat must be kept heeled right over until it points below the port close-hauled course. Then roll the boat upright, getting maximum drive from the sail.

After sailing as close as you can to the boats to windward (shouting "Hold your course!"), roll tack back onto starboard and stop the boat by holding the boom amidships for a few seconds as you step across. You are now in the enviable position of having a beautiful gap under you to power off into at the gun!

Tacking & double-tacking practice:

● Do 10 tacks in your own time up a short leg.
● Sail in a large circle round the coach boat. On the beat do five tacks, or one single and two double-tacks.
● Start with the sailors well spaced out on the same tack. All sailors tack when the whistle is blown. For variety this exercise can be done with eyes shut!

GYBING

Gybing can be tricky and you must practice until it becomes automatic:

1 Prepare mentally, thinking positive thoughts. Try to relax, take a deep breath, and go for it.
2 Check that the plate will not foul the boom or strop.

3. Allow the sail to fill before stepping across, and steer with the tiller behind you.

4. Get sailing, then swop hands and hike.

1. Make sure the top of the dagger-board is below the boom. Sheet in half a metre.

2. Grab the three parts of the sheet and help the boom over.

3. Duck!

4. Ease sheet while stepping across, steering the boat straight.

5. Keep standing and look ahead while you sort your hands out.

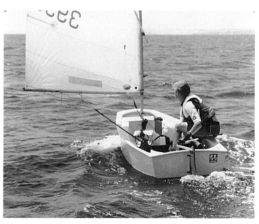

6. Sit down and balance the boat.

3 Pull in approximately 18in (50cm) of sheet, keep the boat level or heeled a little to windward, and bear away smoothly.
4 Lean in and grasp all three parts of the mainsheet about 18in (50cm) above the lower blocks. As the weight comes off the sheet, pull the boom across.
5 Then simultaneously:
● Step across the boat and sit on the new windward side - well aft.
● Move the tiller back to the mid-line to keep the boat sailing straight until total control is regained - you will be steering with the extension behind your back.
● As the boom flies across, ease the sheet a small amount to absorb some of the force.

If you're a lightweight don't try to grab the sheet above the blocks. Concentrate on keeping the boat level as you steer round smoothly, and get across very quickly and up onto the side to balance the boat. Steering straight as the boom crosses and immediately after is vital. Maintaining control and surviving is more important than tight mark rounding

GYBING MISTAKES
Tripping Over The Daggerboard
If you turn a sharp corner at speed with the daggerboard too far down, the boat slips sideways while the daggerboard tip grips the water. The result is a roll to leeward, sometimes bottom up.

Right:
1. Nice level trim looks good at the start of the gybe.
2. Still looking good, but helm is on his knees.
3. He makes a slow recovery, facing the wrong way.
4. The boat is about to nosedive due to poor control when stepping across.

Tripping due to too much daggerboard. Steer straight and step across to balance the boat.

Broaching Loss of control just before the boom comes over, followed by the boat screwing back onto her previous course, is due either to the boat heeling to leeward (leeward chine digs in and steers her back up into the wind), or having the sail too far out making it too heavy to pull over.

Nosediving Caused usually by too much water in the boat and/or the crew not sitting far enough back. Done with style this can result in the boat rolling transom over bow, with the helmsman landing on the sail or even in the water ahead.

STOPPING

You need to be able to stop during pre-start manoevers, making an offwind approach to marks and going for the inside position, or when team racing, which can often become 'Go Slow' racing.

To slow down or stop:
1. Weave about from side to side, using more rudder than necessary.

2. Ease the sail.
3. Sit out over the stern and sink the transom. This increases drag enormously.
4. Luff with the sail eased.

Luff, ease the sail right out, sit out over the transom and sink the stern. To move slowly ahead, lean forward and sheet in just a little.

ACCELERATING

Accelerating is a vital skill to help you get away from the start line cleanly. You must have space below you at the start, having made a slow controlled approach.

Just before the gun goes:

1 Adjust the boat's heading (with the rudder) onto the perfect close-hauled course, and at the same time sheet in the main to the beating position just over the corner of the transom, but do not oversheet.

2 Roll the boat upright or heel it a little to windward, and carefully check fore and aft trim. Don't hit a wave!

3 Apply maximum hiking power if the wind requires it.

SAILING BACKWARDS

This is worth trying now and again, for fun and as practice in getting out of irons. It is an essential skill for confident manoevering at the start when you often need to move back as well as forward under full control.

- Luff and get into irons.
- Try to steer downwind without touching the sail, going backwards on starboard tack. The stern goes in the direction the tiller points.
- Get out of irons, and get sailing as quickly as possible on starboard tack.
- When getting out of irons, lifting the daggerboard will help more than pulling or pushing the sail.

Hold the boom well out for speed-sailing backwards!

6 TACTICS

Tactics is a huge subject. I recommend you read the Fernhurst book *Tactics* by Rodney Pattisson which covers all the situations that crop up. In this chapter we'll just look at the most important parts of the course.

THE START
Start priorities are:
- To get a 'front line' start.
- To have a gap to leeward for acceleration.
- To start at the right end of the line.
- Be busy! Be active! Be dynamic! Be pushy! Be dominant!
- Don't hit people. Stay legal. Starting lines in Optimist races are very congested, and a remarkable amount of boat contact, sail contact, and dubious practice take place. You will survive if you keep awake with both eyes open. Shout in good time if you think somebody will foul you in any way.

Starting techniques
- Spot the line transits on the land, and use a transit on every start.
- Learn to be confident near the line. Sail up and down it; come up to it from below; drop down onto it from above.
- Is there any line bias? In most Championship starts the OOD will lay a line with a 10 degree bias to the port end. If you can dependably make a good port end start, you will gain an advantage over the entire fleet. With a small header you may be able to tack and cross everybody. Practice your port end starting.
- Port end, port tacks are cheeky but Ben Ainslie successfully did two such starts, crossing the fleet both times at the Optimist World's in Argentina. There was a 10 degree bias to the port end, but because the committee boat had a long anchor warp the starboard starters had to start well down the line. Ben was able to tack onto port by the line boat and cross the fleet twice.
- Identify the rate and angle of drift of the slowest possible starboard tack approach. Use this knowledge to get to your planned starting point at the gun.
- Hold your position by filling your sail, gaining a little headway, then luffing until the boat stops. It will then start to slip back, so bear off, get headway again, and luff once more.
- Try to squeeze the boats to windward. This will help keep your nose ahead so your wind is clear and you keep luffing rights. Beware getting so close to the windward boat that it touches and gets stuck alongside you. All you can do in this situation is protest, as he has ruined your start. If you push him back in anger, you're DSQ! Try to stop the windward boats sailing over you. Keep your bow ahead, point high, and hold them back.
- Use double tacking to get into gaps to windward and keep clear water beneath you. Do a 'double' at every opportunity. Starboard tack boats will intentionally be

sailing very slowly, and will not be in a position to speed up much to get you. Under ISAF Rules 15 and 16 they may not alter course without giving you 'room to keep clear'. A loud hail of 'Hold your course!' and/or 'Room please!' may well hold them back.

- Reaching along behind the fleet on port tack with a few minutes to go, hoping to find a way through to the front line needs practice, a good nerve, and a lot of luck! It will not work in a big fleet of top competitors.

- Make sure that you know the racing rules relating to the start perfectly; then make sure everybody round you knows you are in control and they cannot push you around. Threaten the windward boats loudly; tell the starboard tackers to hold their course; demand 'room and time to keep clear' from leeward boats. Be noisy if necessary but keep cool!.

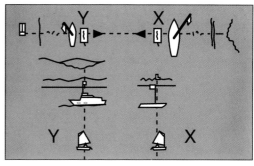

Line transits. Boat X sights the outer end of the line with a church. Boat Y lines up the committee boat with a valley beyond it.

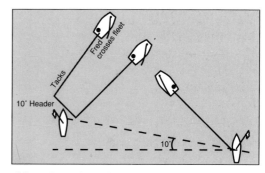

Most championship start lines have a 5-10 degree port end bias. Starting at the port end can give you an immediate advantage over the fleet. With a small header of around 10 degrees, you can tack and cross them all.

Below: A bunch of starboard tackers keep their places close to the line.

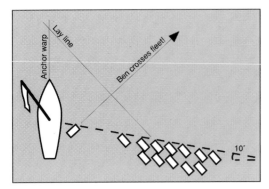

The perfect port end, port tack start. Ben Ainslie in Argentina.

Things to avoid before the start:

- Don't point above closehauled, or you will not being able to bear off and accelerate when you want to and risk getting into irons.
- Don't get too close to boats to leeward. When you are within 4in (10cm), you cannot luff or tack without your transom hitting and you have to sit there until he moves away. By that time you will be in the second row; you may even get in irons and land up in the third row or worse.
- Don't let windward boats foul or sail over you.

General recalls with the black flag rule Do not keep sailing to windward if there is a general recall in a black flag rule start. Immediately stop your boat, sit on the transom, ease the sheet and bear away.

Practicing starting Short line exercises can be used to develop close quarter boat handling, rule knowledge and confidence building. Depending on the number of sailors, set a reasonably short line between two marks with a mark 150ft (50m) to windward for turning. Practice with sound signals at 3 and 1 minutes to go.

- Fight for the starboard end. The idea is to get into and hold the position on the line nearest to the starboard end.
- Fight for the port end. The game is to attempt to get and hold the pin end position. This is virtually impossible, but is good practice for a slow controlled approach, tacking into gaps, and double tacking.
- Place half the group on the line, and then with one minute to go the other half try to get into the front rank. To really congest the line set up a box below the line outside which sailing is not allowed.

THE BEAT
First half of the beat:

- Don't tack too often, and never (hardly ever!) in the first 300ft (100m).
- Follow your race plan.
- Use your compass and sail on the lifting tack.
- Keep in clear air and sail fast.

Second half of the beat:

- Keep away from the laylines and sail the 'middle cone'.
- As the mark approaches, take the nearest tack.

The fleet spreads out as they move into the second half of the beat.

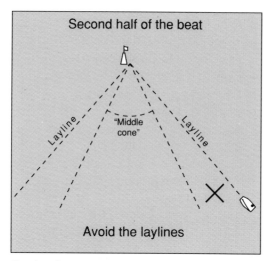

Second half of the beat

Layline

"Middle cone"

Layline

Avoid the laylines

Don't sail on the layline! If lifted, you will overstand. If headed, you will be unable to tack and may overstand later. You cannot avoid boats tacking on you. You have no chance of gaining ground.

THE WINDWARD MARK
Windward mark approach:

1. Get the boat dry before going for the mark.

2. With few boats near, you can sail fast with clear wind right up to the mark. Take your chance with a late approach.

3. In the 'pack', come up to the starboard layline earlier. Sail right through the layline, dipping below boats where necessary until you are sure that you can lay the mark easily. Tack and sail quickly to the mark over the boats backwinding and blanketing one another to leeward.

4. Never tack to leeward or in the middle of the starboard boats on the layline. If you fail to lay the mark you may well have to gybe out.

If you try to luff for the mark and fail you will lose many places -remember an Optimist will never luff round a mark against the tide! If you are going to hit the mark, make sure you get round it then do a 360!.

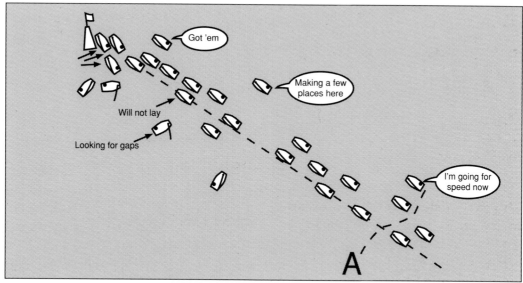

Stuck in the pack? Boat 'A' sails through and past the starboard layline until it has clear wind. It then tacks and sails fast over the line of boats. They are all slowing one another, and some will get in trouble at the mark. Result – a few places gained.

Rounding the windward mark:

- Get onto the run quickly; every two lengths sailed on a broad reach is only one and a half lengths towards the leeward mark. Do however give port tack beating boats room to keep clear (ISAF Rule 16).
- Stay on starboard tack until you have cleared the mark area, and then sail on the most direct route to the next mark (get a transit) keeping your wind clear!

At the end of the reach comes the gybe! Go into this with a positive attitude, and you won't swim.

THE REACH

- Try to sail the straight line course, using a transit if you can get one (ahead or behind).
- Don't let boats go close through your wind. Go high if there is a bunch behind, but only high enough to keep your wind clear. Go low if there is a bunch ahead.
- If you are heavy, ignore lightweight flyers coming up from astern. Psyche them with threats of luffing into passing you well to windward. Keep sailing the direct course. Keep low - let them go!
- Get on the inside at the mark. If you are 2nd or 3rd out, get within two lengths of the mark and then slow down hard and dip round behind the inside boat.

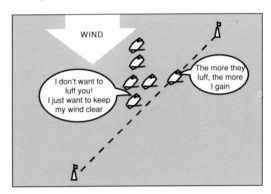

Level-pegging on the reach. If there is no interference, sail straight for the mark. Reach tactics: in this situation the more they luff, the more you will gain.

THE LEEWARD MARK

It is essential to start a beat from the inside position at the leeward mark. From any other position you have no immediate option of tacking clear, and may have to sail for a long time in disturbed air. If you are 2nd or 3rd in, get within two lengths then slow down hard and dip round behind the inside boat. Watch out for boats ahead trying the same trick. If you were 'clear astern' of them at 'two lengths' you have no water rights and will need to do an emergency stop.

THE FINISH
Finish To windward
It is easy to lose places at the finish. You must wrench your gaze from the opposition and force yourself to look at the line. If you specialise in cool finishing you will nearly always make places. As you approach the line, ask yourself "Which end is most downwind?" and then plan to approach that end at speed, preferably on starboard tack. On the approach, be careful you are not being blocked outside the layline. If the port end is nearest, tack onto the comfortable dead cert layline and sail for the pin, shouting loudly to put off anybody who may be thinking of trying to squeeze in between you and the mark. If the starboard end is nearest get over to the starboard layline fairly soon, unless the line boat is taking the wind.

Avoid being sailed up to the port end of the line by boats to windward. When defending, try to sail an opponent out past the layline for the prefered end. When sailing an opponent past the port end of the line, make sure you go far enough past the mark to prevent him getting an overlap when you both tack for the mark.

Finishing on a reach
When approaching a reaching finish keep your wind clear and go for the nearest end. Try to see whether the line has been laid as you approach the leeward mark on the previous round. If the windward end is nearest go for the windward end, luffing if necessary. If the line is square go for the windward end, but if hassled by lightweight flyers drop down and let them luff while you go for the leeward end. If the leeward end is nearest, get down there at nearly any cost.

Finishing on a run
To finish on a run keep your wind clear, sail as straight as possible using a transit, and go for the nearest end. Do not sail by the lee unless you have to stay on starboard for tactical reasons. Gybe and sail faster!

In Position 1, the boat sailing fast on port for the nearest end of the line may pass the starboard tack pair who will sail further before finishing. In Positions 2 and 3, the inner boat is blocking the outer boat from tacking for the line until the inner boat can tack and stay clear ahead.

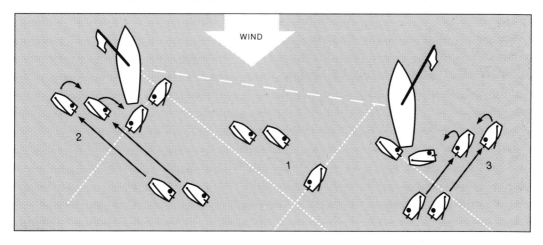

WIND

Part Three
EQUIPMENT
& TUNING

7 MAST RAKE

Mast rake is the most mysterious element of rig control which has probably been blamed for more poor results than any of the other intangibles that go into making a successful race. What really matters is firstly that it is important in balancing the boat, and secondly that the skipper believes his rake is right.

MEASURING MAST RAKE

Technique Mast rake is measured from the mast head to the top of the boat's transom using the following method. Make sure the mast is at the back of the deck slot, and that the step is as far forward as it can move.

1 As most masts are now hollow-topped, hook the tape over the rim at the top of the mast.
2 Extend the tape over the centre of the transom.
3 Take the reading, sighting past the tape to get the highest points on transom and bow in line. Readings are in the range 108 -114 inches (274-290cm). The mast step should be calibrated with marks to show the mast rake so you can adjust the rake afloat.

INTERNATIONAL APPROACHES TO RAKE

The British approach The mast should have moderate rake in medium weather and be raked back in heavy going. This is based on trials which concluded that boats go best with moderate rake of 109-110 inches (277-279cm) in medium weather, with the mast being dropped back to 106-108 inches (269-274cm) in a blow. A well raked sail has a wider chord and is proportionally flatter, with a finer entry and exit than an upright sail with a Bermudian rig. In other classes there seems to be an advantage in rake for upwind work, but this may be due to getting the axis of a Bermudian rig more vertical. The axis of a spritsail is relatively more vertical. The main fault of this theory is that when the rig moves back, so does the CLD, and unless the daggerboard is lifted or the boat kept heeled to windward, unacceptable weather helm results.

Using a tape to measure mast rake.

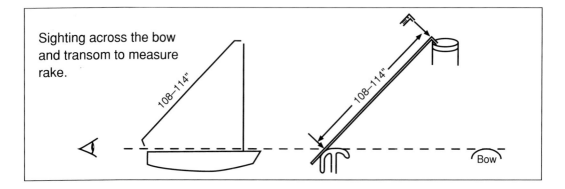

Sighting across the bow and transom to measure rake.

108–114"

108–114"

Bow

The Dutch approach The rake should be adjusted at all times to keep the boom level. This was first propounded by Serg Katz, World Champion in 1984 and 1985, son of the famous IOCA Measurer. He adjusted the rake in all weathers to keep the boom horizontal which has two benefits:

• Minimising boom drag.
• Keeping the CLD of the sail in the same position in the boat, so that balance and feel stay constant.

The mast is raked further forward as the

The Dutch System. Always adjust the rake to keep the boom horizontal, with an approximate boom-end height of 12in.

wind increases, in light weather being 108-110 inches (274-279cm), and in heavy going depending on the sailor's weight and resulting mast bend approximately 110-113 inches (279-287cm). This scheme seems eminently sensible. The CLD does not move and balance can be maintained by boat trim or lifting the daggerboard.

The Argentinian approach Before we became aware of what they were doing, we were struck by the smooth speed of the Argentinians and the fact that they seemed to keep their daggerboards down longer and accept rather more heel. They sail in all weather with rakes of 112-114 inches (284-290cm).

Light winds: Straight mast with 108-110in rake.

Moderate winds: 1-2in mast bend with 109-111in rake.

Strong winds: 2-4in mast bend with 110-112in rake.

The theoretical benefits are:
- A more vertical rig axis.
- More rig height.
- A narrower sail chord.
- CLD well forward, making it easier to balance the boat even with some leeward heel.

The Swedish approach The Swedes have always been very fast. They use a 90 degree square between mast and main thwart to find the mast rake for medium weather, moving the step forward a little for light weather, and back in heavy weather.

This corresponds to unbent mast rakes of 114 inches (289cm) for heavy weather, 113 inches (287cm) for moderate weather, and 112 inches (284cm) for light weather.

Conclusion I like the Dutch theory, but feel it should be applied with more of an Argentinian rake initially. Try keeping the boom nearly level but slightly angled up at the stern in all wind strengths. This will be 110 to 113 depending on mast bend. Lightweights in strong winds, with the daggerboard up, will need more rake – perhaps 109.

THE SEARCH FOR BALANCE

Wind	Weight	Heel	Mast Bend	Daggerboard	Mast Rake	
Force 0-1	all	upright	nil	vertical	111in	282.0cm
0-2 knots	all	leeward	nil	vertical	112in	284.5cm
0-1m/s	all	leeward	nil	raked	111in	282.0cm
Force 1-2	all	upright	nil	forward	112in	284.5cm
3-6 knots	all	upright	nil	vertical	111in	282.0cm
1.5-3m/s	all	windward	nil	vertical	110in	279.5cm
	all	windward	nil	forward	111in	282.0cm
Force 3-4	all	upright	1-2in	vertical	112in	284.5cm
7-16 knots	-35kg	upright	1in	back	111in	282.0cm
3.5-8m/s	-35kg	leeward	1in	back	112in	284.5cm
Force 5	+50kg	upright	2-3in	vertical	113in	287.0cm
17-21 knots	+50kg	upright	2-3in	back	112in	284.5cm
8.5-10.5m/s	45kg	upright	2-3in	back	113in	287.0cm
	-35kg	upright	2in	10cm up	110in	279.5cm
	-35kg	leeward	2in	10cm up	111in	282.0cm
Force 6	+55kg	upright	3-4in	vertical	114in	289.5cm
22-27 knots	+55kg	upright	3-4in	back	113in	287.0cm
11-13.5m/s	45kg	upright	3in	10cm up	112in	284.5cm
	-35kg	upright	2in	20cm up	109in	277.0cm
	-35kg	leeward	2in	20cm up	110in	279.5cm
Force 7-8	+55kg	upright	4in+	raked back	113in	287.0cm
28-40 knots	+55kg	leeward	4in+	10cm up	113in	287.0cm
14-20m/s	45kg	upright	3-4in	20cm up	111in	282.0cm
	45kg	leeward	3-4in	20cm up	112in	284.5cm
	-35kg	leeward	2-3in	30cm up	109in	277.0cm

8 FAST GEAR

The Aim To produce the perfect combination of hull, sail, spars, toe-straps and controls to suit the sailor. The competitor must make his boat as individual and comfortable as his favourite trainers - but first, get a copy of the class rules and read them carefully. You will then know what you can and cannot do.

Hull Buy a new or well cared for Optimist One-Design.
Keep it smooth and clean with sharp edges to the transom and the aft third of the chine. Smooth with 600 grade wet and dry paper, finishing with 1200 grade or polishing paste. Regularly clean and degrease with washing up liquid. Scratches and bangs can be repaired with gelcoat filler.

Always use a well-padded trolley and never let the hull touch anything else. When turning your boat over use two people, one at each end. Turn the boat in one swinging movement through at least 90 degrees,

The perfect combination gives comfortable race winning performance.

putting it down on the gunwale if you cannot turn through 180 degrees in one movement. After use, rinse the hull with fresh water, clean and dry it, and cover the bottom with a soft and preferably padded cover.

Daggerboard Suitable foils are of vital importance to get optimum performance. Like the hull, foils must be close to the minimum weight and should be kept perfectly smooth and clean. The daggerboard controls leeway and acts as the pivot through which your hiking balances the force from the sails. If the board is 'soft' (flexible) it will bend and you will lose 'feel' and drive. However there is an advantage in having a board that bends just a little in heavy weather in the biggest gusts and waves, to act as a shock absorber helping the sailor keep the boat flat and under control. Light skippers need a daggerboard that is more flexible, bending under the lighter loadings they can exert. Heavier skippers need progressively stiffer daggerboards, and sailors over 60kg need a totally rigid daggerboard.

The daggerboard and its box should match. The daggerboard must be accurately made and close to the maximum thickness (say 13.5mm) with no bulges or hollows. The box should be as narrow as possible (say 14.5mm). This ensures:
● The plate will not wobble from side to side in the box, making steering jerky and affecting your 'feel'.

- As little water as possible is trapped in the box. Water in the box adds to the boat's mass.
- Minimal turbulence occurs where daggerboard and hull meet. If your boat has a wide slot, take advantage of the rule that allows the top and bottom opening of the box to be fitted with uniform padding to narrow the slot and make the daggerboard fit more snugly.

The rules allow stops to be fitted in the ends of the top and bottom openings of the

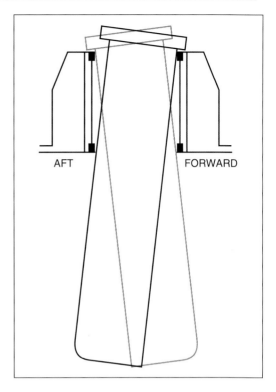

AFT   FORWARD

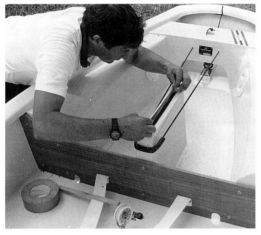

The daggerboard slot should be narrowed to the legal minimum 14mm using adhesive tape at the top and bottom as shown above and below.

case. These prevent the edges of the foil from being damaged, and also to allow you to alter the rake of the board.

The aft bottom stop should be of maximum length (30mm) with a V cut into it to take the foil's edge. Other stops should be no bigger than 5mm. High density rubber glued in place with Sikaflex is very satisfactory.

The daggerboard's rake can be controled with a loop of elastic cord fixed to the sides of the case by two eyelets. This allows the board to be raked forward, back, or held vertical in the box to improve balance.

> *Beware! Hot sun can warp foils. Keep them out of the sun, or if possible in padded bags.*

Rudder The rudder has a lot of work to do. It transmits the feel of the water and signals the state of balance of the boat to the helmsman. It is the means of controlling the boat. To perform these functions it is essential that both rudder blade and head are as stiff as possible so there is little or no twist between tiller and blade. Cut-away rudder heads are more prone to twist than conventional ones.

Use padded bags to protect the foils

The rake of the rudder blade is critical. Too much rake and all steering movements become heavy and tiring. Too vertical and 'feel' is lost, as is the paddle effect of the swept back blade which is essential for boat handling at slow speed on the start line. Every possible shape of rudder has been tried to minimise drag and increase efficiency. The main drawback of any tapered tip design is loss of slow speed control. My feeling is that a simple rectangular rudder with a rounded forward corner is probably best. The rudder head frontline should be mounted as far from the transom as allowed under the rules (near to 40mm).

Tiller 600-650mm seems about right. Too long and it gets in the way, too short and the steering gets heavy.

Tiller extension This should be as long as possible to a combined maximum of 1200mm. Do keep an eye on the universal joint. It can fail quickly - disaster!

Toe straps Get the right position and tension. I favour quite tight straps to maximise the rate of response of the boat to crew movement and reduce knee bend.

Hiking pants Padded trousers or strap-on pads make hiking much more comfortable. They should not be worn in light weather as they make it harder for you to move easily and feel what the boat is doing.

Mast For speed and high pointing, all sailors need as stiff a mast as possible. Optimax, Optipart and Giulietti masts are of similar stiffness and are among the best. You need a pin step and low friction mast thwart sleeves to minimise rotational resistance. In very rough seas with a heavy crew the mast plug can collapse due to the high loadings, and it is worth having a cup fitting in your box for such conditions. The mast thwart sleeve must hold the mast snugly athwartships, allowing maximum legal fore and aft movement (3mm). The mast step must have a very snugly fitting track to prevent any side-to-side movement, but the step adjuster must allow the step to slide back and forward over the maximum permitted range (3mm).

Sprit tackle with British cleat position.

A good system with roller-bearing blocks using the British cleat position.

This cleat grips laid-rope better than plaited-rope. The standing part of the tackle goes through the hole in the cleat.

The sprit tackle must be strong, with low friction blocks, a good handle and the cleat positioned where it can be adjusted easily. There are two commonly used cleat positions. The Optimax position is below the lower band, and has to be adjusted by a bouncing technique from a standing position, pushing downwards on the handle with all your body weight. Using a long wire from the mast block to the lower block at gooseneck level minimises windage and turbulence over the sail luff. It also possibly stiffens the mast a little by acting as a stay, although this effect is negated as soon as the mast bends. Most Continentals accept that this is the best system, and expect top sailors to use it. I suspect it results in insufficient and inaccurate sprit adjustment in the junior fleets and probably also in the seniors. Light and inexperienced sailors cannot hope to use this system.

The British cleat position is some 16in (40cm) below the mast block. This allows the sailor to lean forward, sitting on the buoyancy bag/tank/side deck, and pull down on the handle. All sailors find this system easy to use. There is some windage penalty, but in most cases this is more than made up for by better sail setting.

Sprit tackle with Continental cleat position and cup mast step.

Top sprit tackle block The attachment to the mast is a common site of gear failure, which inevitably results in retirement. Patent methods should be viewed with suspicion. A simple solid stainless steel hook is pretty safe. Suspect riveted fittings; check screw tightness regularly; carry a spare top block and a length of kevlar for rapid repairs.

Sprit & vang cleats

Aluminium clamcleats work well, but can slip with thin, plaited rope; when cleating the rope, shove it into the 'V' to improve grip. Optimax use stainless steel 'V' cleats which grip positively, but wear the ropes quickly.

Adjusting the sprit one-handed while steering.

Adjusting the sprit two-handed, using full body weight.

Vang The vang rope is subject to considerable wear. It should be fairly heavy, with a stopper knot or a bowline on the end to help you grip it. It is essential that the mast and boom rotate together, or sprit tension and sail setting will change when you tack. The vang cleat can help this by standing out from the mast as far as possible. As packing pieces are not mentioned in the rules they are presumably not allowed, but a deep cleat with an in-built becket serves well. The becket must be modified to minimise sideways movement of the rope - a Clamcleat can easily be grooved for this use by a small round file. The mast retaining tie-down rope is important. Pass it over the vang cleat, but do not tie a knot where it can catch on the cleat and do not pass the tie down around the mast several times. Both can stop the mast rotating when you tack, changing the sprit tension and the sail shape.

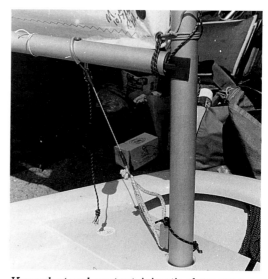

Vang cleat and mast retaining tie-down rope. Note that the knot is in the wrong place - it should be tied back to the eyelet on the mast thwart.

Double-purchase outhaul rigged on a modern boom (Optimax).

This strop spans the middle half of the boom. Note the outhaul cleat is positioned forward for ease of adjustment when the sheet is eased.

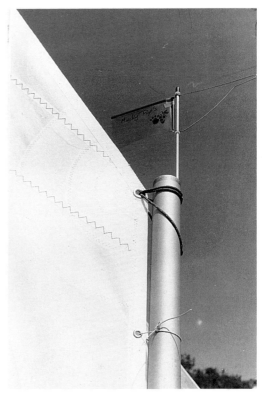

The throat is 8mm from the mast; the top mast tie has a 5mm gap.

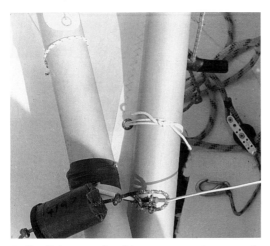

Luff sail ties must be thin, strong, and go round the mast twice for accurate adjustment.

Top Ties Top Ties must be very strong as they take the enormous thrust of the sprit transmitted down the headrope. If they stretch your leech tension varies, and the throat may move illegaly far from the mast (more than 10mm). The Optimax system is efficient but difficult to adjust. If the rope used is too heavy the knots will not pull down into the aluminium plugs and will slip. Use Kevlar or Sectra of 3mm compressed diameter, and replace ties for each major event and heavy weather races. Watch for wear where the cringle rubs and where the ties go into the mast. Some Argentinians use Optimax masts but do not use the tie plugs, passing the ties through the holes, around the flag and back out again, securing and adjusting them with simple, dependable and easily adjustable knots! The Italian Top masts have returned to simple top ties, using long thin cord which goes round through the cringle and mast holes several times, making it possible to adjust the tension very accurately for optimal sail setting. The Optipart system seems to be functional, with removable eyelets which lock in place with the flag. The ties are easily adjusted by knots.

Boom Boom stiffness is essential to keep the sail flat in heavy weather. A bendy boom will slacken the leech in gusts, but will result in the sail becoming fuller and more uncontrollable. Mast, sprit bend and sail cut allow the leech to fall off adequately in gusts, complementing the use of sprit and vang A strop spanning the middle half of the boom will stiffen it usefully, but must not extend more than 10cm from the boom.

Strong jaws are important to promote total rotation of boom with mast.Vertically wide, tight jaws can cause the leech to be too tight in light weather, by not allowing the boom to lift. None of the jaws currently available are perfect, and the best would be a very tightly-fitting, narrow jaw. It is possible to cut away the upper inner part of a standard jaw to allow the boom to lift without appreciably affecting the jaw's grip. Surfers' wax applied to the jaws and mast helps sticking.

All modern booms have special end fittings allowing minimum-friction double-purchase outhauls to be rigged. The rope must be Kevlar.The outhaul cleat should be fitted in the middle of the boom where it can be reached easily on most points of sailing. A boom uphaul loop (tack diagonal tie) must be fitted to the jaws. It slips over the pin on the front of the mast above the band, controlling luff tension and length. To raise the boom and slacken the luff, simply twist the loop a few times before hooking it on.

A well set-up boat allows you to adjust the outhaul quickly and easily when racing.

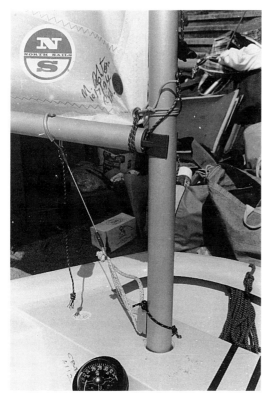

Boom jaws must grip the mast tightly. Note twists in the tack diagonal tie.

Mainsheet This should be attached to the boom span with a quick-release clip. Ball-bearing blocks only should be used. The upper becket block should attach to the clip with a length of kevlar or wire, to minimise the amount of mainsheet needed. The rachet block must be dependable and the switch to engage the rachet must not jam or slip. The mainsheet should have a clip on one end to engage on the becket of the top block (on for a triple purchase, off for a double purchase). A lightweight sheet is best in light weather, but beware freshening wind! Use or carry a pair of gloves.

Painter IOCA rules require at least 8 m of 5 mm buoyant rope. Attach to the mast foot, tie a loop 40 cm up the line (on which to tie painters of boats being towed astern) and stow under a buoyancy strap amidships. Praddles, sandwiches, water bottles, and so on should all be stowed amidships and not in the ends of the boat.

Compass Not essential, but it can be a very useful tool when sailing at sea with few landmarks to help spot the shifts. Two types are popular - the spherical Silva and flat Suunto.

The Silva is usually mounted on the vertical face of the mast thwart in the mid-line. It has a simple mounting bracket which enables it to be removed when not in use. It operates accurately at all angles of heel, and has a magnified black card with a Degree Scale in white and a Tactical Scale in yellow. The Tactical Scale is read behind the sight line nearest the windward side of the boat. The scale is designed so that when the boat tacks through 90 degrees the difference between the readings on the two tacks is 10 - eg. Port 8, Starboard 18. On starboard tack, when the wind lifts and the boat points higher, the reading on the tactical scale decreases. When headed the reading increases. On port tack the opposite is true: when lifted the reading increases, when headed it decreases. Mark the sides of the bulkhead with a reminder! Note that each unit on the Tactical Scale is 18 degrees, so even a half unit shift is quite significant.

The Suunto is a flat compass with a relatively large card divided into red, green and black coloured sectors. It has a conventional 360 degree scale and is best mounted on a removable bracket behind the daggerboard box. This allows the sailor to adjust it easily, and look down onto the compass. In this position the compass is very close to the mainsheet, but does not seem to snag. The card is set up by pointing the boat 'head to wind', and then rotating the compass in its mount until the long reading line corresponds to due north (000). When you bear off to close hauled on port or starboard tack, the big pointer will line up between a red and a green sector. When the wind lifts the line moves into the green; when headed, it moves into the red.

Simple, no numbers! By seeing where the line points in relation to the eastwest line on the card when you're sailing along the start line, you can see tell which end is more to windward. The disadvantage of this compass is that the boat must be sailed flat - the compass will not cope with more than 15 degrees of heel.

The Suunto compass is ideally sited by the daggerboard case.

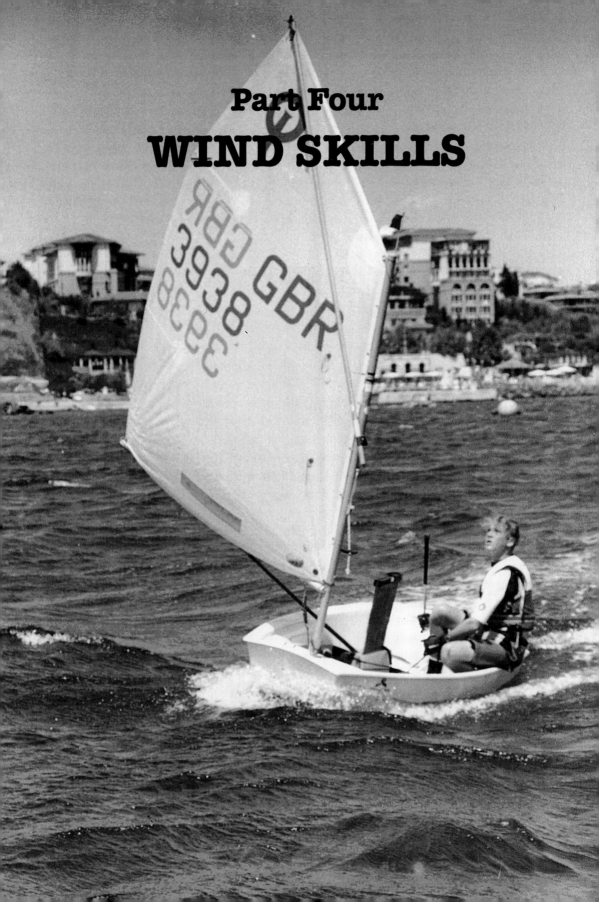

Part Four
WIND SKILLS

9 SEEING THE WIND

With a bit of immagination the wind can be visualised flowing over and around everything. It slips over water, jumping from wavetop to wavetop, with little eddies in the troughs. It rushes along in jet streams high above the planet, tearing the clouds into jagged mackerel scale shapes. Lower wind is slowed and deflected by friction as it rubs over land and sea, mountains and forests, farmland and lakes. The wind finds the easiest route to flow round obstacles, just like water moving over rocks in a stream.

Imagine yourself sailing a course with headlands, moored ships, valley inlets and a patch of forest near the water. Use the wind bends to get to the windward mark first, and always sail towards the centre of a bend.

Feel the wind on your face. Is it blowing harder on one cheek than the other? Can you feel it on your ears? When it cools both sides equally, you are facing dead upwind. Hear the wind. Look upwind and move your head slowly from side to side. When you can hear it whistling equally in both ears, you are looking dead upwind.

See the wind on the water. You will see ripples being blown downwind. On smooth water these ripples are exactly at right angles to the surface wind. On rougher water you will see most ripples on the tops of waves where the wind strikes. As the surface wind varies the ripples in each group will be from a slightly different direction, but they can still give a good overall indication of the wind. On fresh water in strong winds foamy lines can be seen going dead downwind on the water's surface. Seen from a height these can map out the air-flow over a lake, showing wind bends.

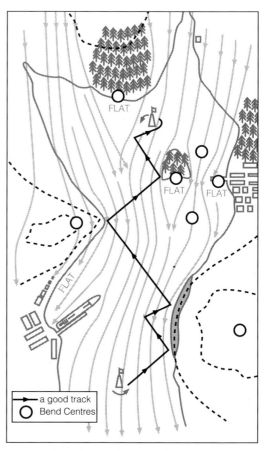

When sailing in an estuary or river you have to imagine how the wind blows over hills, through trees, or past ships lying at an angle to the wind. Always sail towards the centre of a wind bend.

Squalls & gusts These can be seen as dark patches on the water, with bigger waves sometimes breaking with white flashes of foam. A line squall may be seen rushing down from upwind, looking like a dark smoking line right across the course: a sign of doom! Look down from a cliff at the patterns gusts make when they hit the water. First you see a dark circular patch where the gust strikes. Then dark lines run out from it in all directions as the supercharged wind explodes outwards.

In gusty weather keep an eye open to windward. When you see the telltale dark patch of a squall approaching, try to see whether it will pass ahead and to leeward or behind you. If it passes ahead, the wind escaping from it will head you; tack and you will get an enormous lift. If it passes astern you will be lifted well! It's not so good to be caught dead downwind of a big gust. You get the struggling but no lift, so if you think a squall will hit you squarely consider tacking to get to the side of it before it strikes.

Anticipating the wind Besides looking at the course and imagining how the wind will blow over it, look at the clouds. In flat areas the lower clouds are of vital importance in predicting the wind. Under a puffy white cumulus cloud the air is going up, so there will be less wind and it tends to back (shift to the left). As the cloud passes, faster air gusts down from the higher 'gradient' wind to replace the hot air rising in the cloud. This wind will be stronger and veered (shifted to the right). So as a cloud approaches, sail on port as the wind drops and goes left; after it passes, sail on starboard through the fresher veered wind. Look for gusts coming down through the blue gaps between these clouds (stronger and veered). Watch out for rain falling from dark clouds; wind usually comes down with the rain.

Sails bend the wind Imagine the airflow around a beating Opi sail (dia., p62). A boat on the same tack to leeward or a little behind will be headed by the turned wind and will slow down. A boat close to the windward quarter will also be slowed down, both by striking the wash and by being headed by the deflected wind. A boat on the other tack crossing the stern of our boat will get a lift from the turned wind.

If you are sailing in 'dirty wind' that has been deflected by someone else's sail, don't hesitate - tack and use the lift! Matters are much worse if you are in the dirty wind of several boats. This is the position when you are in the third rank at the start. It is essential that you get onto port tack and wriggle out, going under the

Gust passes astern - expect a lift on starboard.

Gust passes ahead - tack when you reach it for an enormous lift on port.

WIND

GUST

Gust lifts you squarely - no advantage, only hard work.

When reaching, the deflected wind will make it difficult to pass close to leeward.

When light wind kiting the air flows from luff to leech, and the drive rolls the boat to windward.

In heavy weather downwind the air flows from leech to luff. The drive heels the boat to leeward which is balanced by hiking out and back.

starboard tack boats to the right side of the course. Because of the turned wind from their sails you will go really quickly, and hopefully eventually find some 'clean' air.

In team racing, when close covering, your aim is to get the opponent squarely in your backwind, tacking to keep covering him if he tacks. This will slow him down considerably, and he can be slowed even more if you oversheet as he loses speed. Don't slow down more than he does or he will tack and go through you!

When reaching, the deflected wind will make it difficult for anybody to pass close to leeward, as several boats in a group will produce a big block of slow-moving deflected wind. On the run an Opi sail has a different flow pattern in different wind strengths. Groups of running boats produce very damaging areas of slow-moving turbulent wind to be avoided at all costs by boats ahead and by beating boats - never beat through groups of running boats, for even if you avoid the wind shadow the wash will get you!

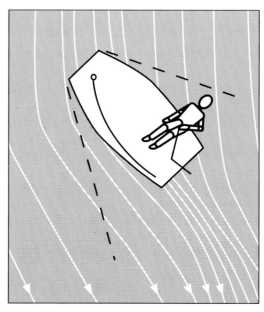

Wind theory This is fascinating and essential knowledge for every sailor. I strongly recomend that you read *'Wind Strategy'* by David Houghton (Fernhurst Books) which covers the following vitally important concepts:

Surface wind refraction; Stable and unstable air; Coastal effects; Convergence and divergence; Typical lake winds; How tide and water temperature changes affect the wind; Gusts and lulls, downdrafts and squalls; Sea breezes; Messages from the clouds; Obstacles in the wind; Surface water drift; At the Regatta - How to make wind predictions.

WINDSHIFT SAILING

By keeping awake and using windshifts you can sail a shorter course upwind, covering the distance to the weather mark more directly and leaving those fast guys who went the wrong way struggling far astern!

Spotting Shifts

1 Watch your boat's heading on the shore ahead. When you are lifted you can point 'higher' up the shore; when backed 'lower'.
2 Watch the boats around you. If you seem to be getting lifted above the boats to leeward and the boats to windward are being lifted above you, you are on a lift. If the boats to leeward of you suddenly seem to be pulling ahead and you are dropping down, while climbing in relation to boats to windward, you are being headed!
3 Watch clouds, wind on the water, yachts to windward.
4 Use your compass.

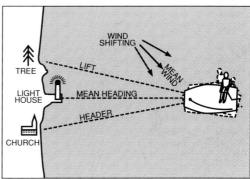

Watch your boat's heading when sailing towards the shore or a fixed object.

Left:
In a lifting wind, boats to leeward drop back and down; windward boats move ahead and open up; opposite tack boats do badly. In a heading wind, leeward boats lee-bow you and pull ahead and upwind; windward boats drop down behind (tell them to tack, then go yourself); opposite tack boats do very well.

Getting to know the wind pre-start

You need to find out:

1 The frequency of oscillation of the wind. Wind is seldom steady, oscillating from side to side with a frequency that may be as short as 30 seconds or as long as 30 minutes.

2 The mean direction of the wind. You need to know your compass headings when close hauled on each tack, when the wind is from the mean direction.

3 Wind bends on the course. On the way out to the race area, keep awake and try to confirm whether or not a bend exists by sailing past a headland, or running down through the course area from the windward mark.

4 Wind shifts expected during the race, due to meteorological changes or sea breezes. The expected shifts can be worked out in advance by the weather forecast and inspired guesswork on the morning of the race.

Use the compass Once in the start area, sail upwind on one tack for ten minutes or so checking the frequency of oscillation and the maximum lift and maximum header. From these you can work out the mean wind direction and the compass settings/readings that represent the mean upwind course on each tack. The importance of this is that when you are on a lift and the wind starts to back slowly, you must be careful not to tack until the wind and the upwind course have swung 'back' past the mean direction. In very shifty weather, if you lose sight of the mean headings on each tack you will be tacking on small headers and losing out badly.

After the start it is easy to glance at the compass to check that you are sailing on, or higher than, the mean upwind course for that tack without loss of concentration on speed. If you see that you are heading below the mean course, then take the first opportunity to tack! Result: Faultless shift sailing; magnificent first mark position.

Of course it is not as easy as this. Not only are starboard tack boats preventing you from going where you want, but the wind itself does not always 'play the game'.

Don't rely only on the Compass

Use your eyes as well. You can only depend on the compass for your tactics in winds that oscillate from a steady mean direction. Do not blindly sail on compass readings in the following circumstances:

- Wind bends on the course. The compass may be useful away from the influence of the bend.
- Meteorological changes in wind direction, such as a front crossing the race area or the sea breeze coming in. Such wind direction changes will make nonsense of mean wind estimates. If you do not spot that the wind is changing permanently, and take it to be just a

good lift, you will end up sailing on a long, slowly lifting tack when it would have been better to take a short hitch towards the new wind direction and then lay the mark. Keep a good eye on yachts to windward. What wind have they got? Where is it coming from? When the wind steadies again, by all means reset your compass but be cautious about trusting it absolutely.

- If the frequency of oscillation of the wind is longer than the duration of the windward leg, you will sail one beat on one part of the wind cycle and the next beat on another part. In these circumstances your compass is of little value except to give an idea of where you are in the cycle.

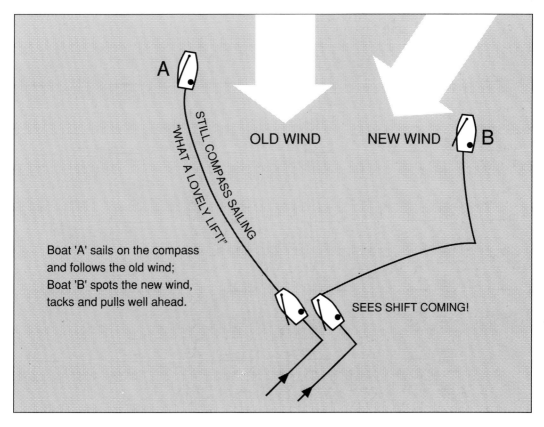

A

OLD WIND   NEW WIND   B

"WHAT A LOVELY LIFT!"   STILL COMPASS SAILING

Boat 'A' sails on the compass and follows the old wind; Boat 'B' spots the new wind, tacks and pulls well ahead.

SEES SHIFT COMING!

Part Five
MIND & BODY

10 MENTAL FITNESS

WHY SOME PEOPLE WIN

In the top twenty of any national squad you will find accomplished and experienced sailors who all have perfect boat handling skills, comprehensive knowledge of tactics and the racing rules, immaculate boats with good new sails, and all sail fast! Why is it then that certain people win nearly all the time? It could be that winners have better mental skills, and in all sports great attention is now being paid to mental fitness.

Objective evaluation Winners are able to evaluate their own feelings and performance before, during and after competition. They develop the ability to examine their performance, identify strong and weak points, then use that knowledge to plan changes in tactics or training to correct matters. They are also capable of identifying damaging emotions before, during or after a competition.

Clear planning Winners are able to set achievable training goals covering specific processes which require work (eg. bailing to windward). They set performance goals (eg. sail the beat perfectly; plan tactics for every situation), and also set outcome goals (eg. win a race in the National's, Top Ten in the World's).

Highly confident Winners are totally confident of their ability. They are sure they can sail a perfect race, and winning or not winning is subject only to the vagaries of the sport. They have perfected techniques to maintain their confidence and block out failures.

Stress management Winners are aware of their levels of stress, and can use techniques to keep that level optimum for tip-top performance. If you are too stressed or too laid-back performance suffers.

Mental rehearsal Winners are able to visualise their sailing so effectively that they can practice starts, mark rounding and other tactical manoeuvres without going afloat.

Psychological race enhancement Winners have a developed ability to visualise each different part of a race, to examine it and the emotions felt at that time. You can use visualisation techniques to come to terms with a race in which you made a major error by visualising a succesful outcome. If you lost your cool at a particular time in a race, you could visualise the lead-up to the incident, trying to pinpoint exactly what threw you.

Concentration Winners have developed the ability to concentrate deeply for long periods. In addition, a characteristic of Olympic competitors is their strong will to win. To excel at that standard of competition, strong motivation is essential. These competitors have the overpowering ambition to be 'better than all the rest'. They

don't want to lose, but must avoid the negative fear of losing. This drives them to try harder, hike further and longer, concentrate more, sail accurately and carefully, think fast, keep mentally calm, stay physically flexible, and Work!

Further reading At this point I recommend you read the mental fitness section of 'Mental and Physical Fitness for Sailing' by Alan Beggs (Fernhurst Books). It covers this subject in two sections.
1. 'Brain Sailing' stresses the importance to boatspeed of allowing yourself to sail in a state of relaxed awareness, by diverting your attention to the sensory experiencies of sailing. Techniques are introduced which you can use to develop the sort of creative, intuitive sailing which is a characteristic of gifted sailors. It also covers performance assessment and goal setting.
2. 'Mind Sailing' covers confidence building, stress management, and

concentration maintenance, including coping with distractions and re-focusing when things go wrong. It covers relaxation, centering, compartmentalising, harnessing emotions, visualisation, mental rehearsal, psychological race enhancement and positive thinking.

MENTAL TOOLS
Training and racing log As an aid to self-coaching, on the evening after a race day thoughtfully and honestly fill in a Race Analysis Sheet (page 95). The most important entries will not be mast rake, sail used or foil rake, but your assessment of your performance. What went well and what aspects of your sailing need more work? The next step is to do something about it! Keep these sheets in your log, and as you achieve your training and medium term aims your confidence will improve with your results.

Scrapbook Keep this for results, pictures, sailing instructions and so on, and when you've had a bad day thumb through and see how much you have improved and remember your good races. Keep a 'scalp' page and enter the name of every top sailor you beat. If you can beat them once you can do it again!

Video If you've had a good race or series, try and get a copy of a video of it. Every time you watch it you will get a confidence boost. It will also help you visualise yourself sailing well.

Talk Take every chance to talk to top sailors about how they've achieved their successes, and imagine yourself in their shoes.

'30 Second Bubble' This is a useful way of coping with things that happen during a

Are you confident, calm and assertive enough to be a winner? Well get the bow up and start that boat moving!

race. Shut out anything that has happened over 30 seconds ago. Concentrate only on the present and immediate future as if you are in a bubble of time.

The bubble will help you exclude from your mind everything that has or will happen outside that time. Forget the hassle; let it go, settle down, control yourself and get back to concentrating on simply sailing fast!

Look forward and out Another useful coping technique. If something happens, try to forget it by concentrating hard on sailing your boat fast purely by feel, keeping your eyes forward and out, scanning only the water immediately ahead and to leeward until you have control again.

Examine your emotions An example is fear. What are you afraid of exactly? Is it a logically justified fear? Is it stiffening your muscles or interfering with your breathing? Fear is a natural safety mechanism, making you 'freeze'. It's natural; you can't do anything about it; so accept it but be firm that you are not going to let it rule you or interfere with your race.

Desensitisation to aggravating factors If you get up-tight when people shout, get all the other members of your training group to shout during exercises. After coping with friendly shouting, strangers shouting in competition will not be so daunting. Similarly competitors have to learn to accept decisions of 'on the water judges', however inept or wrong they may seem. This can be practiced by introducing a number of unjust and erroneous rulings into training that competitors have to accept.

Self affirmation and buzz words Look in the mirror on race day, look yourself in the eye, and say "You're good - you've beaten them all before". Say "Great!" when things go right, "Good tack!" when you do a good one, "Slippery!" as you slide swiftly downwind. When you pull off a cunning move, say "Sneaky!", "Another one bites the dust!", or something similar. It will keep you hyped up and flying. Build up a selection of buzz words to use at different times in the race.

Arousal If you are feeling lethargic after the five minute gun or after several general recalls, get yourself zapping by imagining something really powerful, frightening and here! Everybody has to find their own electrifying image it might
 be a ghoul, a crackling high voltage cable, or similar. Try making a noise to suit! They'll think you 'bananas' until after the start - when you explode away.

Controlled aggression This can be effective afloat in getting your own way. In using this technique it is essential that you can keep your mind cool and clear, and do not infringe the rules. Be very careful that you do not 'commit a gross breach of good manners or sportsmanship' (IYRR 75.1). This clearly excludes the use of bad language in your dealings with other competitors.

Assertiveness Younger competitors and girls need to develop assertiveness, based on a sound knowledge of the rules. A loud and clear early hail, and a conspicuously waved B flag can work wonders. Don't let the aggressive kids have it all their own way!

Singing and whistling Good for you when racing. They help you relax and distract the opposition. The secret is to develop the ability to do it without thinking about it!

Executioner's eye, gunslinger's smile This is a phrase I picked up from a book by Dennis Conner. I have always found it useful when in tactical battles with an opponent. It is also handy in helping you counter the psyching out and winding-up talk that goes on in the dinghy park at big events. If somebody is trying to get you worried, give him the gunslinger's smile and look him over for execution!

11 THE PERFECT BODY

HEAVY OR LIGHTWEIGHT?

Weight is of great interest to Optimist sailors and their parents! Usually they have no need to worry, for the Optimist is a remarkably weight tolerant boat. An experienced heavyweight can confound opinion and turn in winning performances in all weathers. A demonstration of this was given by Ben Ainslie at the 1992 UK National Championship, which he dominated in both light and heavy weather, weighing 63kg (10 stone). For average sailing conditions the optimum sailing weight would probably be 35-56kg (6st to 8st), but each weight group has its own particular problems of rig tune, trim, movement in the boat and technique which have to be solved for top performance.

World Champions 1989 – 2000

Weight range 34 – 59 kg
(5 st 5 lb – 9 st 4 lb)

Height range 150 – 183 cm
(4 ft 11 in – 6 ft 0 in)

Top 10 in World Championship

Average weight for 10 years
46 kg (7 st 3 lb)

PHYSICAL DEVELOPMENT

Optimist sailing spans late childhood and early adolescence. During this time the steady growth of childhood leads into the 'growth spurt', a two year period of very rapid height gain, after which growth slows down as adult height is reached. Individuals develop at very different rates: early developers may be physically up to four years ahead of their peers in height and strength, but their growth stops earlier. By 18 they have often been passed by guys who were the smallest in the class at the age of 12! In the Optimist class it is common to see these well co-ordinated and strong early developers dominating the younger age groups, but they can get too big and heavy in their final Optimist year. By this time their later-maturing friends are getting stronger and are reaching optimum weight.

Growth risks Identifying the growth spurt is important, because during this time the mechanical advantage of muscle groups change, making an individual much more subject to injury. This problem can be seen most clearly in some thin children who go through an awkward, clumsy phase during their growth spurt, when the bones seem to grow faster than the muscle needed to control them and the nervous system's ability to control them. All young athletes in training are particularly at risk of sustaining injury to the growing bone ends, ligaments and muscles when exercising strenuously. The most common and well known problem for sailors (as for footballers) is Osgood Schlatter's Syndrome, a painful swelling on the upper end of the tibia where the patella tendon attaches to a growing area of bone. Hiking hard (or kicking a heavy football) can lead to strain and considerable inflamation at this point, as the muscular action of the quadriceps tries to pull the tendon off the bone. Treatment is rest and no hiking (or kicking) until it settles, sometimes for six months!

Boys & girls Adolescence in boys brings a sharp increase in height, weight, shoulder width, muscle, bone mass and strength. They become leaner, losing the body fat of childhood. Boys have the peak of their growth spurt around about the age of 14, but it can be as early as 12 or as late as 16. Adult height is usually reached at about 17 or 18. In girls, adolescence brings first an increase in height, followed some six months later by a weight increase. Their strength does increase at this time, but much less than the boys and most of the weight gain is in fat rather than muscle. Girls have their growth spurt peak around the age of 12, though it may be as early as 10 or as late as 14. By 15 to 16 a girl will

normally have reached full adult height. Fortunately, in the final Opi year (aged 15) girls have had their growth spurt and strength gain, without the full weight gain of late teen years. Boys on the other hand are in the middle of their growth, and have not yet developed the muscle of later years. It is thus still possible for boys and girls to compete equally.

Sexual development and an increase in hormone levels can cause physical, mood and behavioural changes in adolescent children as well as mental and emotional preoccupation. The onset of menstruation must be treated sympathetically, but it need not necessarily affect performance in training and competition.

12 PHYSICAL FITNESS

FITNESS HELPS

Physical fitness is seldom necessary for successful performance at club level, but becomes increasingly important for good results at regional, national and international level. Fitness can help your sailing in four main ways:

1 It helps to prevent you from getting tired. Racing, particularly in heavy weather, can be exhausting. If you are fit you will be able to sail harder and keep fighting longer than the next man.

2 It speeds up your recovery between races. The demands of championship sailing are often much greater than those encountered in a single event. Incomplete recovery between races held 'back to back' or on successive days can lead to your getting more and more tired, and less capable of doing your best in the races at the end of a hard series.

3 It keeps you sharp mentally. Tired, unfit sailors find concentration difficult. This affects their ability to make quick correct tactical decisions, and their performance suffers. Physical exhaustion makes it much harder to keep mentally positive and cope emotionally with events during the race.

4 It prevents injuries. Most injuries occur when the body is tired and cold. When you are fit, you are much less likely to injure yourself when racing hard.

TRAINING REQUIREMENTS

Size & weight Training requirements vary with a competitor's size. Sailors weighing less than 35kg should aim to develop stamina, hiking and arm strength. Sailors weighing over 50kg need to develop flexibility, agility, balance and co-ordination, although stamina is still needed in heavy weather.

Time on the water Hours on the water can of course make a useful contribution to fitness. If you could sail three times a week for a half hour or more in winds of Force four or above, you would certainly develop good sailing fitness. However it is impractical for most Optimist sailors to do this even if the wind were suitable. In the summer only 30% of days in Britain have winds of this strength or more. More winter days have suitable winds, but with a winter race training programme extra stamina and fitness training is needed. This can be provided by sport and fun in and out of school.

- Flexibility
  Stretching and warm-up exercises; Wild dancing.
- Agility
  Surfing; Windsurfing; Skateboarding.
- Balance
  Football; Rugby; Hockey; Netball.
- Co-ordination
  Badminton; Table tennis; Squash; Golf.
- Reactions
  Wild dancing!

● Strength
  Circuit or rugby training at school.
● Stamina
  Distance running; Jogging; Cycling;
  Swimming.

WARM-UP & FLEXIBILITY

Warming-up Warming-up before
training and exercise avoids injuring cold
muscles and ligaments. Ideally you should
warm-up and warm-down before and after
all strenuous sailing. Before races it is often
worth warming-up twice - on shore and just
after the 10 minute gun. After general
recalls a warm-up routine can not only help
the muscles, but will also help to wake you
up and get you ready to fight.

Flexibility This refers to the range of
movement which is possible at joints. You
needs a fair ammount of flexibility to move
around a boat smoothly and easily. Some
girls have most amazing natural flexibility,
while some boys, particularly the muscular
early developers, can be remarkably stiff.
Flexibility can be improved by regular
gentle stretching exercises. For these to be
effective, the end of the range of movement
must be reached and the position held for a
few seconds. It is important that such
exercises are always carried out in a
controlled manner. Violent, rapid or
bouncing movements should be avoided
as these are likely to be ineffective and
may lead to injury.

> In exercises 3-8 take limb or trunk
> gently to the end of the range of move-
> ment and hold position for 5 seconds;
> repeat 3times; do not bounce in the
> end position.

FLEXIBILITY
First Warm-Up:

1 Running on the spot -1 minute; or Step-
ups - 15 leading with right leg, 15 with left.

2 Arm circling -15 forward, 15 back.

3 Back flexion stretch - Lying on back with knees bent. Draw right knee and nose together using hands to help. Repeat with left knee, then both knees.

4 Quadriceps stretch - Lie on face, bend left knee. Reach behind with the left hand, hold left foot, bring it to buttock and increase stretch so that knee just rises from floor. Repeat with right.

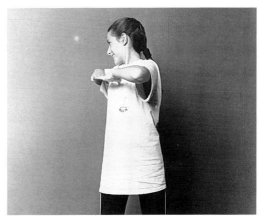

5 Shoulder stretch - Standing feet astride, hands in front of chest, arms horizontal, press elbows backwards then forwards.

6 Trunk twist with head turning - Start as for shoulder stretch; rotate trunk and head to left; repeat to right.

7 Side bend - Standing, feet shoulder-width apart, press one hand on hip while stretching the opposite arm over the head at 45 degrees. Repeat other side.

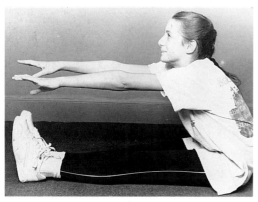

8 Sitting stretch - Sitting with both legs outstretched, gradually lean forwards from the hips. Do not push towards the feet by rounding the back and leading with the head, as this can cause back strain.

9 Back extension stretch - Lie on the floor face down with hands palms down under the shoulders, and forearms alongside trunk. Push up the trunk keeping the hips on the floor. Relax in this position, then slowly lower.

WARMING UP AFLOAT

Why? It is good practice to get afloat well before the start of the race in order to check conditions, decide how to play the first beat, set the boat up for the winds found on the course, check out the favoured end of the start line, and so on. However, being on the water early and not being very active can mean that the body becomes quite cold by the time the race is due to start. This can be even more of a problem if races are postponed or there are recalls. A short 'warm-up' can help a lot!

When? Usually just after the ten minute gun. If there are recalls or postponements, repeat at every ten minute gun.

What? Try some of the following, for one or two minutes:

1 Rapid shadow boxing with a circling rather a jerking movement.

2 Running on the spot, in a press-up position with arms on transom or gunwale.

3 Arm circling, forwards or backwards.

4 Hand and neck circling, in both directions.

5 Press-ups as in 2.

A SAILOR'S CIRCUIT

For those of you who want to go for the Olympics in ten years, and for folks who can't stand school sport, here is a 'Circuit' that you can do a number of times a week at home. It incorporates exercises for your back and hiking muscles. Make sure you warm-up and stretch before starting the circuit. Find your exercise targets by performing each of the exercises for 30 seconds and record your scores, taking a 1 minute rest between each exercise.

Next session, go through the exercises in turn, doing each exercise the target number of times. Repeat the sequence three times over. Time yourself and note it down. Each time you do the circuit, try to improve your score.

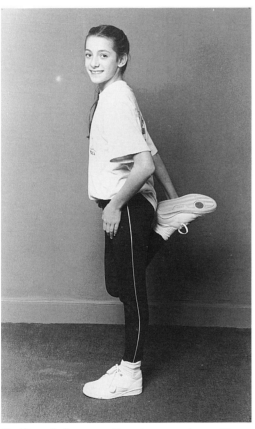

1. Quadriceps. Stand on one leg with the other bent to a right angle at the knee. You can hold onto something if it helps. Bend the weight-bearing leg slowly, by about 20 degrees only. Hold for 1 second. Then straighten the leg again. Repeat 5 times, then change legs.

2. Running on the spot. Use vigorous arm movements. Lift feet about four inches (10cm) off the floor. Count each time the left foot touches down.

3 Sit-ups with twist. Lying on back with fingers holding ear lobes and knees bent to 90 degrees, sit up to touch knee with opposite elbow.

5 Wall sits. With knees and hips bent to 90 degrees, 'sit' with back against a wall and arms folded without sagging for 30 seconds.

6 Back flexor/abdominal strengthening. Lie on back, knees bent 90 degrees with feet flat on the floor and not under a bar or bench. Hands on ears, tighten abdominal muscles, keep lower back flat, slowly raise head and shoulders off floor until in half sitting position. Then slowly lower to starting position. Breathe out on raising and breathe in on lowering.

4 Back extensor. Lie on stomach. Keeping the knees straight, lift one leg while keeping the hips in contact with the ground. Hold in the air for a moment then slowly lower. Repeat 5 times, then change legs.

7 Walk round your feet. Start in press-up position, and using arms only 'walk' in a circle around feet. If you don't have room for a full circle, go from side to side through 90 degrees and count the 'cycles'.

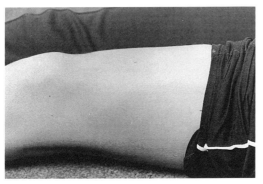

8 Isometric medial quadriceps. Sit with legs straight, hands placed just above kneecaps. Contract quads, particularly the part on the inside of the thigh. Count to five, then relax.

9. Press-ups.

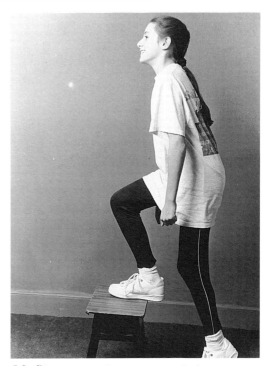

10 Step-ups. On to a stout chair or bench. Step up with one foot, follow with the other foot, lower first foot to floor, bring the other foot down, repeat.

STAMINA

To build up stamina you should aim to jog, run, cycle or swim for at least 20 minutes three times weekly. A fanatic could try an 'Aerobic Trail'.

- Jog - 5 minutes
- Squat thrusts - 30 secs
- Run at half speed - 2 minutes
- Press-ups - 30 seconds
- Run fast 100m, jog 100m - 2 minutes.
- Bent knee sit-ups - 30 seconds.
- Run at half speed - 2 minutes
- Run on the spot, high knee raise - 30 seconds.
- Run at half speed - 2 minutes.
- Run fast 100m, jog 100m - 2 minutes.
- Jog - 2 minutes.

HIKING

A paper by Dr Frank Newton (ex RYA Hon. Medical Advisor) points out the high incidence of knee problems in young sailors (common in older sailors too!). He suggests this is due to a dangerous hiking style. Most sailors hike draped over the gunwale with knees bent and body in an 'S' shape. Dr Newton says that hiking 'Laser style' with knees bent no more than 20 degrees is less likely to cause knee injury. This is because the sideways pull of the main quadriceps muscle is balanced when the knee is straight by the pull of the medial quadriceps muscle. This muscle ceases to work effectively when the knee is bent more than 20 degrees. The result is that the kneecap slips outwards and rubs on the outer ridge of the femur, causing wear and pain.

Optimist solution Try to hike like Laser sailors. Set your straps tight and high in the boat, and sit out with knees bent no more than 20 degrees. With practice this will be no more agonising than hiking the conventional way, and you will have the benefit of being further from the water and less likely to be hit by waves. The special exercises for the medial quadriceps (circuit No.1 and No.8) are well worth doing. Do not train with weights! While your back is growing the ends of the bones are soft. Using weights in training can permanently damage your back, leading to back pain and weakness all your life.

EATING FOR ENERGY, FLUID FOR FITNESS

Energy is stored in your body as something called Glycogen. It is important to have as much of this as possible in your body when you arrive at a major competition.

In the week before the competition:
1 Eat plenty of carbohydrate. Complex carbohydrates = bread, cereals, spaghetti, rice, potatoes, beans, peas, lentils, root vegetables, fruit (bananas are brilliant), biscuits, cerial, muesli bars, cakes, puddings, sweet and fruit yoghurts, fruit juice. Simple carbohydrates = chocolate, confectionary, jam, marmalade, honey, glucose and of course sugar (added to drinks and breakfast cerials).
2 Cut down your training.
3 Avoid large meals. Eat little and often, and increase your fluid intake.

At the regatta Before the regatta find an 'Energy Bar' that you like and take enough to save the need for shopping. Chocolate bars contain mostly 'simple carbohydrates' and only give a short boost. Muesli bars

are much better. On the night before the regatta, have a light meal. On the morning of the regatta, have a light carbohydrate breakfast with plenty of fluids. Complex carbohydrates are best. Allow yourself several hours to digest food properly before racing starts. Try to eat simply during the regatta. Choose foods you are used to, avoid shellfish and undercooked or spicy food, and drink plenty of non-alcoholic refreshment.

Drink During the event, and in training, sip fluid regularly. Before competing drink 250-500ml cold water; urine formation is reduced during exercise so 'pit stops' will not be necessary. At hot venues you will perspire more and will need to drink more. Avoid salt tablets - you don't need them. Nor do I recommend isotonic high calorie drinks for sailing events, because they cause a surge of blood sugar that can

increase your production of urine. Stick to water, weak squash or dilute fruit juices.

After races Take fluid and some carbohydrates, preferably 'complex', starting as soon as possible after the race finishes. At the end of the day's racing, start refuelling immediately with a complex carbohydrate to give the glycogen stores as long as possible to build up. On coming ashore the feeding process will continue.

JET LAG
Problems Jet lag can result in a competitor being tired during the day and unable to sleep at night. If the time difference between home and the ragatta venue is considerable, sufficient time must be spent there to acclimatise before racing starts. Adjustments can be started in the days before travelling, during the flight, and in the first few days after arrival.

Flying west You need to delay your body clock, which you can start doing on the days before departure by going to bed and getting up as late as possible. During the flight, set your watch to the new local time and try to sleep during the 'new night' and stay awake during the 'new day'. At the venue, force yourself to go to bed at the right time, and if you wake early 'lie in' and keep quiet until the proper time to get up. Try to take the size and type of meals that you have at home, at the times you normally take them but at local time.

Flying east Going this way you have to advance your body clock.Go to bed and get up earlier for a few days before departure, and adjust to local time as before when getting on the plane. At the regatta venue you will have difficulty waking and will feel tired in the morning, but will not feel tired when local people are turning in. Force yourself to get up, and do some sort of gentle exercise in the mornings (walking, jogging or gentle sailing). Go to bed at the local time you would at home, resting even if you can't sleep.

SEASICKNESS
How to prevent it:
1. Take seasickness tablets. Try different kinds at home until you find one that doesn't make you feel ill. Take them in the dose and at the times described in the information sheets. In particular, take them on the night before as well as on the day of racing.
2. Take sweets with you and suck regularly - Barley sugar, Peppermint, Glucose.
3. Keep busy, keep sailing, particularly if you start feeling tired which is one of the first signs of trouble. Don't stop and bob up and down!
4. Between races, stand up and keep your eye on the horizon rather than on the waves or the tossing boat.
5. Keep warm – cold people are sick quicker! Do onboard warm up exercises.
6. Think positive. "Great weather for surfing!", "I can hack this!", "Let's get down to work!"; not "Yuk! I hate this. I'm going to be sick soon!".
7. If all else fails, you can be sick and win yacht races. Many of the best sailors feel uneasy in a confused sea, but they don't let it beat them. Chuck up and get on with the race! Keep your mind on the job and don't let it damage your efficiency and resolve to race effectively.

So long as you keep busy, seasickness is unlikely to be a problem.

Part Six
PARENTS
AND COACHES

13 FOR PARENTS

A PUSH TOO FAR?

We all know the popularly held image of the Optimist parent, towering over a crying child on the slipway, shouting "I told you to go left up the beat!". Of course the vast majority of Opi parents are not like that, but the few that are give the rest a bad name. We all want our child to do well, and get excited when they succeed and downhearted when something goes wrong. The average parent at a regatta is:

1 Ambitious for his child's success.

2 Has invested heavily in gear, clothing, petrol and accomodation, and has spent many weekends doing nothing except follow the Optimist circuit.

3 Can think of a list of things he or she could be doing elsewhere.

4 Is cold, is unable to see what's happening afloat, and is cheered then depressed by garbled progress reports from those parents with high powered telescopes.

5 In general feels their child could and should do better.

Obligation & failure None of the above points will help the child be a better sailor, but they can give the child feelings of obligation and failure, adding to the stress of competitive dinghy racing. The young sailor in question may be ambitious and talented, or of average ability and motivation. He or she may sail for a number of reasons that have not occurred to the parents:

1 Independence afloat.

2 Because friends sail.

3 Good fun messing about in boats.

4 Been pushed into it by parents, but would much rather "Listen to music, get into my computer, go riding, play mini Rugby".

The reasons why As parents we must look at why we take our children sailing. Is it frustrated ambition on our part, or because we feel we have something worthwhile to pass on to the child? We can seek to inspire our children with our enthusiasm and delight in sailing, but have to allow them to find it for themselves. They are at an impressionable age and will certainly do what we want them to do, but the time will come when they will lose interest in the sport if they are not finding their own reasons to continue with it. We must be sensitive to our children's attitude to competition, and to their aims in sailing and their everyday lives. Very few people are able to win national and international championships or the Olympics. We must support the children at the standard they wish to compete at, rather than constantly implying that they should be doing better.

PARENTAL SUPPORT

Physical - Home, security, accomodation.

Emotional - Understanding, insight, comforting, supportive, loving father/mother figures, dependable, predictable, consistent, realistic, inspirational.

Financial - Funding for boats, equipment, clothing, travel, accomodation.

Logistical - Transport to home club for training, open meetings, national and international events, arranging accomodation, feeding afloat and ashore.

Bosun - Checking, repair, maintenance, launching and landing assistance.

Facilitator - All the time.

A BAD RESULT

- Don't start listing what went wrong as soon as they come ashore. Let them do the talking if they want to; if they don't, try to avoid discussion of events until emotions have cooled. Try and work out your child's recovery time. After a bad race competitors of all ages need a time to recover emotionally, before being able to think clearly and analytically.

- Give some thought to your reaction to seeing them sail the worst race of their life. How long do you need to recover before you can:

1 Be civil to anybody?

2 Bring yourself to look at the child?

3 Speak to the child?

4 Control your body language (hunched shoulders, glowering face, irritable movements?).

5 Discuss the race objectively, without your disappointment being transfered to the child?

The child's view Your child may well know more about sailing than you will ever do, and will certainly know more about what happened afloat. They may be bitterly disappointed by their result, know that you will be disappointed, and will be wretched

before you utter a word. In such circumstances I have seen young sailors who have not wanted to come ashore to face their parents' reaction.

Try not to say a word; give them a squeeze, and put their boat away. Later that night after relaxing and eating you will both be in a better frame of mind to take a logical and realistic look at the problem. Show them that whatever happens you love them and think they are great!

Treat them in the same way whether they win or lose, and try to act naturally on the drive home even after a total disaster. Do be sensitive to their needs, and considerate of their moods. Give your child space to develop as an independant person. Try to work out what your child really feels about competing - is it just to please you? Praise and emphasise the good things your child did in the racing. Build up their self-esteem, and beware the careless comment that may put them down.

- Do have realistic aspirations for your child.
- Don't use sarcasm at any time.
- Do encourage your children to take part in other sports.
- Don't fall out openly with other parents, or upset your child's opponents.
- Let the coach do the coaching; do not undermine him.

Parents with coaching ability

Be careful not to limit your child's ability to use his own knowledge and judgement. The sailor must be encouraged to develop the ability to coach himself, to analyse his performance objectively, and plan the aims of his own training. He must decide his own tactics after listening to the opinions of 'experts'. Knowledgeable parents should seek to work with the coach. If they do not agree with aspects of his teaching or sailor-handling, they should talk the matter over quietly in private. A coach who is also a parent must not favour his own child, and must ensure that his child relates to him only as a coach in the sailing environment when he is working. Otherwise he will lose objectivity.

INTERNATIONAL CHAMPIONSHIPS

Parents are a valuable and necessary part of an international sailing team. The coach will of course take responsiblility for training and racing matters, but as at home the competitors will benefit from the support of one or more of their parents who can fill the following functions:

Manager/team leader -Responsibile. for air flights, accomodation, communication with the organisation, going to meetings, living with the team and looking after their needs such as food, laundry, health care, transport, and off the water activities.

Bosun - Transporting and packing boats, checking and setting up charter boats to suit each sailor, modification of boats during measurement, ongoing repairs, help afloat during training, launching and recovery assistance, security.

Helping the coach Most parents will of course come as spectators, but almost invariably their children will appreciate their presence even if they do not acknowledge it. It's always good having supporters about, and the team will be lifted by them. If there is a serious problem with a child, their parent's unique experience can also be invaluable in sorting matters out.

A parent may be asked by the coach or team leader to keep an eye on the notice board for changes to the sailing instructions, collection of results, notices of protests against competitors, notices of meetings, and so on. Parents can also be very useful in helping to get boats measured, being careful to minimise the effects of this stressful time on the competitors. Parents must however defer to the wishes of the coach if he considers that a sailor would benefit from less parental contact. It is sometimes difficult for a parent to appreciate that in the highly charged atmosphere of an international event their tensions are being passed on to their child.

14 THE PERFECT COACH

Optimist coaching is a rewarding experience, from the sheer fun of a group of kids surfing and shouting their way downwind in a Force six to the agony and pure thrill of supporting talented competitors in an international regatta.

Different standards Coaching to national standard involves repeatedly going over theory until it is absorbed. Boat handling and basic exercises must be practiced until boat control is reflex control, and confidence and ability are high. Top national sailors will mostly have the knowledge to get to top international standard. Their challenge is to use that knowledge effectively. This requires a different kind of coaching in which encouragement, facilitation, and technical support become more important, as the competitor develops his own sailing and self-coaching skills.

The step between top national and top international standard is enormous. Sailors fail to grasp the amount of work required. The Coach is Teacher/Trainer, Friend, Performance Analyst, Motivator, Disciplinarian, Counsellor, Facilitator, Technical Expert, Researcher, Manager/Administrator, Publicity Agent.

Teaching Teaching advanced racing knowledge and skills is a prime function of an Optimist coach.

Training This involves setting up appropriate exercises afloat and ashore to aid development of top racing skills.

Planning The racing year must be planned around major targeted events to enable the racers to reach peak performance at those times. Every year's training programme should cover all aspects of dinghy racing. With national team selection trials in April/May and major national and international championships in July/August, courses in the northern hemisphere should run from early January to April, with polishing sessions before the Championships.

Talks & Discussions A young person's attention span varies from about 5 minutes at age ten to 20 minutes plus at age fifteen. Plan to break talks with questions, demos, pictures or a quiz to maintain interest. Talks must be short and simple, but not childish. Complex concepts must be explained clearly and simply using drawings, model boats, and demonstration. Lengthy boring topics like the racing rules can be covered in 10 minute blocks, with revision during debriefs when actual incidents are discussed. Be prepared to abort a talk and go afloat if the audience's concentration is lost.

Use 'Speak Show Do': describe something, demonstrate it, and then get

them to try it. In their first year younger sailors may not retain or fully appreciate the significance of some information, but after going over the subject for a couple of years the same sailors become capable of giving the lectures! Use regular recall to fix things in the mind. This can be done before starting on the main topic of the day, or can be brought into the 'debrief' periods. It is very effective when top sailors comment and contribute as much as possible. Plan talks when sailors are fresh - first thing, or after lunch. Advanced topics can be covered at the end of the day as an option for more mature competitors.

Communication Do your very best to prevent any sailor losing face during training. Don't use sarcasm, make jokes, or encourage laughter at the expense of young or sensitive individuals. Don't use questions that imply that a sailor has or may have made an error. It is better to avoid starting questions with "Why?" as this implies criticism. Try starting with "What? When? Where? How much? How many?". Help competitors to express how they are

getting on and what they think about something, by developing an effective questioning technique. Start with general questions and then focus down to more specific questions using simple words. If you ask a question you must listen carefully to the answer, think about it, and use their words to shape the next question. This will increase a sailor's awareness and will help them formulate new answers and ideas. Above all keep the fun in all aspects of training and competition, with varied activities and lots of breaks for snacks.

Typical Training Day Timetable:

09.00 - Get changed, rigged and ready to sail.
10.00 - Recall of practical and theoretical points from previous day.
10.05 - Talk/discussion.
10.25 - Racing Rules (one rule or incident).
10.35 - Briefing and goal setting for the day.
10.40 - Launch.
10.55 - Boat handling.
11.25 - Starting exercises.
13.00 - Ashore.
13.15 - Debrief/video/lunch.

13.30 - Talk/discussion/rules.
13.50 - Briefing.
13.55 - Launch.
14.10 - Boatspeed work (in pairs).
14.30 - Match racing.
15.45 - Race (long).
17.00 - Ashore, change, boats away.
17.20 - Debrief/video/tea.
17.40 - Optional: psyching!
18.00 - Home.

Briefing/debriefing Before going afloat it is important to outline the aim of the session, and to detail the activities that will take place.

On returning ashore each activity will be discussed, and their values assessed. Each sailor should be encouraged to say how they got on. Any incidents can be discussed and lessons drawn. The debrief is probably the most important session of the day, for here fun afloat can be used to illustrate important points of theory in an easily understood way. At the end of any session it is vital that the sailors are able to have a chat with you privately to air a problem or to sort out an idea.

GETTING TO KNOW THE SAILORS

- Spend a lot of time together in training, and learn how they react afloat and ashore, body language used, and so on.
- Always be available for a chat about anything at the sailing club, at home, and on the phone.
- Get to know each sailor's parents, home situation and ability at school, in order to be aware of outside influences.
- Recognise an individual's response to the stress of competition, and help each person to find ways of coping.
- Recognise how best to give support

when things go wrong. Emotions can be difficult - anger, frustration, or disappointment must be controlled or contained or performance will suffer.
- Get to know a sailor's social skills - the ability to fit in a group and interact happily. Shy loners need help to establish their place in the group.

PERFORMANCE ANALYSIS

Identifying strong & weak points by the coach - Use careful observation.

By the competitor - Use post-race questionaires and target charts. The coach may spot unrecognised weaknesses.

By another sailor - Use a pair-training buddy.

Aim setting Watch for competitors who set themselves unrealistic goals, and are never satisfied as a result. Encourage realistic goal setting.

Confidence Encourage logs or scrapbooks - with each good result confidence will grow. Some sailors, particularly girls, find starting difficult due to pushy, over-confident children. Tell them they're good, remind them of successes, do exercises in which they have to get to certain points on the line under pressure. Make sure they know starting rules backwards and can shout "Protest", show a flag, and keep concentrating on the start all at the same time. Promote confidence in being able to sail in any weather, any time, anywhere, confident that there is nothing to fear from wind and water.

Praise Look for things to praise in all sailors, but be selective with praise in top performers - praise effort and performance more than results.

Believe in his/her potential, but do not expect faultless, perfect and mature sailing all the time. When an error occurs, don't hold back praise for the good sailing. Remember that sailors do not mean to make errors; they will recognise them and will feel deeply disappointed with a poor result. We have all been in the situation where we have known exactly what to do, but in the race everything went wrong. It is one of the marvelous things about sailing that conditions vary constantly and victory is seldom certain. The place of the coach is to support rather than criticise or bawl them out!

PROMOTING SELF-COACHING

Encourage the sailors:

● To think independently and objectively.
● To analyse their own strengths and weaknesses, and to use that knowledge to establish realistic training and long term aims.
● To develop on-going performance analysis skills to enable them to monitor progress towards those aims.
● To identify negative emotions and cope with them in competition.

TEAM SPIRIT

● Try logos on tee and sweatshirts.
● Try a flag or logo on boats, sailing kit, bags, cars.
● Use a team coach-boat, easily recognisable.
● Have a war-cry - "Oggie! Oggie! Oggie!".
● Work on your personal image too.

DISCIPLINE

Practice the behaviour you expect from your sailors; be fair, considerate, and understanding. As a coach you have to be judge and executioner, and after a long day's training you may be tired and not as discerning as usual. Certain activities, the worst of which is team racing, cause emotionally charged incidents to occur between tired sailors. Summary rulings can lead to frustration and anger, whether or not the ruling was correct.

Minor transgressions are usually best overlooked. More serious cases may be called over to the coach boat. Usually a quiet, understanding but stern word will settle matters. If there is an argument between two squad members, call both over to the boat and sort matters out. Speak quietly and be totally fair and impartial.If it's clear that the sailor cannot control himself, suggest that he sits out the next exercise. The ultimate sanction would be to send someone ashore, but I have never needed to do this. Remember that emotional outbursts may be due not just to immediate circumstances, but also to hormonal changes of puberty, shyness, parent problems, relationship problems, money worries, or school worries.

Facilitator/researcher/technical expert/performance analyst

● To help the sailor understand the sailing instructions, cope with protests, deal with aggravations.
● To be an information gatherer on tides, forecasts, expert opinion, new ideas.
● To provide or find the answer to any relevant questions, providing the information top sailors need to consider in their challenge for top results.

COACHING SCENARIOS

- Long term coaching of a top national, area or club group of competent racing sailors over several years. Ideal group size: 8-12.
- Short term coaching of a team in preparation for a major event.
- Individual coaching of an outstanding top sailor. Most Olympic sailors are coached individually, or share a coach with up to two other competitors. This is unusual in the Optimist class, although some parents try to fulfil this role.

Long term coaching With groups of 12 sailors or less, this is the most satisfying and productive arrangement. It is unusual for a sailor to be at the top of the Optimist class for more than four years. Long term coaching over this period will be very beneficial. A good coach will encourage his racers to listen to other experts and collect information from every possible source. Such coaching is best done on a club or area basis. Sailors should be invited to join the training group when they are capable of completing a club race, they want to race,they are capable of self-rescue, they have suitable equipment.

An elite coaching group may be gathered by invitation for National Team or Squad sailors who are keen to work with that coach, strongly motivated to improve their performance, and committed to training regularly which usually means that geographical constraints limit participation. This type of group should train for a period of at least six months.

Short term coaching Short term coaching of a team preparing for a major event usually takes the form of 2-4 .weekends and a week spent at the championship venue immediately before the event. It is likely that you will know the sailors fairly well, but the training periods should be used to get to know much more about them, their attitudes to the competition, their parents and their peers. Work with each sailor, identifying their aims, and their perceived strengths and weaknesses. Develop personal plans for the training period, and re-assess by phone mid-week after each training session. Build up an idea of how they react to stress, successes and failures. Develop a support plan for each sailor.

Afloat, use pair-training for tuning, speed and windshift spotting practice; sailing up opposite sides of the coarse to confirm wind bends and sea breeze effects. Work on starting (particularly port end), acceleration, mid-line judging and mark rounding. Match racing develops boatspeed and race winning skills. Team racing is fun and should be used for relaxation, but it can become excessively aggressive and should be tightly controlled.

Generally, make sure that whatever you organise allows individuals to cover their own training aims, and don't neglect to gather tidal and meterological information for the area where the racing will be held well before the event.

Boat measurement This is a traumatic time, even if nothing is found to be wrong. You must be present to talk with the measurers about any perceived infringment. Check with an up to date copy of the class rules to make sure that the interpretation is correct, or that alternative interpretations may be as valid. An appeal to the chief measurer should always be considered. It is good for morale to get measured as early as possible, but there is always the risk that you will get involved in that year's controvertial rule interpretation. These are always sorted before the event, but can worry competitors for days. Keep cool, positive, and confident in your handling of measurement problems, and your sailors will stay cool too. If modifications are needed to the boats or their gear, delegate this if possible to a competent parent. You must keep on top of other measurement questions, keeping the team occupied and supporting the anxious skipper.

Focus on the competition Go over the sailing instructions with the sailors as soon as they are available, and make sure they fully understand them. Recall important and unusual points at subsequent briefings. On the morning of the first race keep the team focused and positive with early boat checks and rigging; plus a briefing/discussion covering tide predictions, wind, possibility of shifts, as well as the programme and arrangements for the day. The sailors must be given information clearly and accurately before going afloat. Give your advice, but do not order your team to all "Start at the port end and sail up the left side of the course". The predictions of even top international coaches should not be trusted by sailors to the extent that they follow the plan whatever happens. A top sailor is in a better position to see what's going on in a race, and should be encouraged to think for himself and decide what to do without fear of criticism when he comes ashore.

Afloat Use the coach boat to get out to the race area an hour before racing starts if possible, towing the team if the wind is light. Check wind and tide at both the start and windward mark area if possible, and report back to the squad by - which time they will have done their tuning and shift tracking runs. Take a look at all sails, and help readjust rigs or reassure the racers. Anchor and discuss tactics and ideas. Withdraw outside the race area when required by the sailing instructions, and watch the start if possible from the favoured end of the line.

It is almost impossible to see what is going on in big fleet racing, so during the races try to relax and keep tracking wind and tide. After the race, the guys who have done well will come alongside first. Congratulate, feed and water them, and find out what happened, where they started, what the wind did, and how their speed was. Suggest they sail off to eat, drink and have a pee. Eventually the day's disasters will come in. They may or may not want to talk things over. You should know them well enough to know what to do. Feed them, fix anything, and offer them the chance to come aboard for a rest. In good time for the next start, get them doing warming up exercises before focusing on the next start.

Going ashore After the last race of the day, put up the flag, cruise up to each sailor in turn, and praise/encourage as merited. Give them something to chew and drink, and tow them in if the weather is light. Don't try or encourage discussion of the day's racing until several hours have passed, to enable the competitors to come to terms with their results and look at their performance objectively. Ask parents to respect this rule; ideally the parents should not discuss the race with the competitor until after the debrief. The boats must be checked and packed away and the sailors changed, showered and fed.

Protests Before heading home the coach should have a beer and wait for the end of 'Protest Time', to check for protests against the team or alterations to the sailing instructions for the next day.

Protests are daunting for a young competitor at his first international event. Help by getting the protest form and rule book, and calmly talk over the incident. Guide the sailor to the most effective form of presentation of the case, both on paper and before the committee. Just by being present during the wait for the hearing, you will be a comfort and help your team member.

Debrief Hold the debrief for the day's racing after supper at a pre-arranged time. Each race should be carefully analysed and race winning points noted. The coach should then speak to each competitor in turn privately. This gives the chance to go over any negative feelings. Hopefully perspectives will change and a more positive attitude will be achieved. Parents with experience and insight may contribute to the debrief, but you must be aware of possible inhibiting or attitude modifying effects they will have on their offspring. This can be assesed in the pre-regatta training period; if in doubt about any parent, all should be excluded from the debrief.

COACHING EQUIPMENT

Coach boat This must be easily manoeuvrable with light steering and smooth throttle control. A rigid bottom inflatable type boat is most suitable at sea, although cases can be made for other boat types in particular circumstances - for instance a Zodiac type soft bottom inflatable is seaworthy, versatile and easy to carry when deflated. Your boat must have ground tackle that will hold in all conditions - at sea an anchor of adequate size with at least 15 feet (4 metres) of chain and plenty of warp. It should also carry a waterproof tool kit with a plug spanner, a spare set of plugs, a spare prop and cotter pins, an emergency starting rope, an emergency fuel can and a tow line.

Race marks You will need at least two buoys, with anchors and warps. Small Dahn buoys with flags are practical.

Sound signal Cheapest and easiest is a whistle.

Sail battens Use them to signal start sequences.

Hand-bearing compass/flag Use for wind shift tracking.

Watertight box Use to carry a selection of the following according to coaching circumstances: VHF hand-held radio with watertight sleeve; clipboard and paper, pens and pencils; knife, pliers, screwdriver, small adjustable spanner; plastic tape, sailpalm, needle and thread; adhesive sail repair tape and scissors; shackles, sail ties, length of light Kevlar line;

IYRU Rule book; sunglasses, sunscreen; dictaphone in watertight sleeve; wind guage; binoculars.

Tide stick To guage the flow of the tide.

Loud hailer To decrease strain on the vocal cords.

Video camera In watertight bag or box.

For major events Spare foils, mast, sprit tackles, etc; food and drink for the troops; a large team or national flag.

VIDEO AFLOAT

Uses To demonstrate good technique and tactics; as an aid to tuning; as an aid to visualisation and mental rehearsal.

Disadvantages Can be boring; taking pictures from a small boat in anything but calm weather can make you feel sick; when used to demonstrate errors, it can lead to the competitor concerned suffering a loss of self-confidence.

Practical points Who will do the shooting? It is difficult to coach and shoot video. Fortunately in the Optimist class there seem to be plenty of experienced parents who will shoot under your supervision. It is of course essential that the person using the camera is familiar with it. A stable boat gets better pictures, and bigger boats are best. The committee boat is a perfect platform for shots of start and finish.

Clingfilm is useful to protect the camera from rain or spray.

A good waterproof housing is invaluable.

Shooting tip In a smaller boat stand at the point of minimum movement, usually about a quarter boatlength from the stern, and try to keep the horizon at the same position in the frame. Do not use full Zoom.

It will magnify the camera's movement. Never shoot into the sun except for artistic effect. Shooting angles should be either at right angles to the direction of movement, or from ahead/astern.

Replay First time, show the video without comments. Second time, make comments that are positive, constructive and not pointed. Invite sailors to comment on their own tactics. Invariably they will know what they should have done, and don't need anybody else to point it out to them!

MONITORING RACE PROGRESS

Both in training and in a major event it is useful to record positions at every opportunity. This helps you to keep in touch with each individual's progress. It is easy to watch those that are doing well, but lose touch with what is happening to the others. Later you will find it very handy to be able to show a disappointed sailor that they did at least do a brilliant third beat. A good method is to record windward mark placings for various promising sailors eg:

Windward mark placings.

Jim			
1stWdwd	2ndWdwd	3rdWdwd	Finish
40	32	36	28

Target Chart A Target Chart is useful as a means of evaluating a competitor's perceived ability and self-confidence. It is handy as a starting point for discussing training aims. Each sector concerns a particular skill. Sailors assess their ability in that skill on a score of 1-10 and shade in the sector accordingly. You can also use a Race Training Analysis Sheet - see opposite.

RACE TRAINING ANALYSIS SHEET

Report No: Event: Date:

Skipper: Sail No: Boat Name:

Sailmaker: Sail Cut: Sail Age:

Wind Strength (steady? shifty? gusty?):

Sea State (smooth? choppy? swell?):

Waves (direction? effects? technique used?):

Luff Tension (number of twists on tack diagonal tie):

Luff Shape (convex? straight? concave?:

Top Tie Gap: Tack Tie Gap: Luff Tie Gaps:

Outhaul Tension/Foot Shape:

Mast Rake:

Daggerboard (vertical? forward? back? raised? how many cm?):

Best Trim (upright? heeled to leeward? heeled to windward?):

Balance (weather? lee? neutral helm?):

Speed Upwind:

Speed Downwind:

Specific Problems:

Answers/Comments:

RACING NOTES

Pre-start: Start:

1st beat: Weather mark:

Good points: Problems:

Finish: Comments:

FURTHER READING

Write or phone Fernhurst Books for a free colour brochure or check our website www.fernhurstbooks.co.uk

Fernhurst Books, Duke's Path, High Street, Arundel, West Sussex, BN18 9AJ, Tel 01903 882277. email sales@fernhurstbooks.co.uk

We particularly recommend the following books for Optimist racers.

The Rules in Practice by Bryan Willis. Explains the current racing rules. Each common situation is shown in a drawing and the author explains what each boat may, must or must not do. Also contains the current rules for reference.

Tactics by Rodney Pattisson. A gold medallist explains how to out-manoeuvre the rest of the fleet at the start and on each leg of the course. Also includes Match Racing & Team Racing.

Mental & Physical Fitness for Sailing by Alan Beggs, John Derbyshire & John Whitmore. An Olympic coach and psychologist explain how to get fit for sailing and how to tune your mind for competition.

Wind Strategy by David Houghton. Explains how to predict the wind on the racecourse. Gives examples of wind planning at a number of regatta venues, plus summary charts to laminate and take afloat.

The Secrets of Sailboat Racing by Mark Chisnell and Neal McDonald. The 180 things you need to do to win.

Sailpower by Lawrie Smith & Andrew Preece. Explains the theory of sails, hulls, rigs and foils to the non-technically minded, and shows how to use the theory to sail faster.

Knots & Splices by Steve Judkins. How to tie knots that stay tied and make splices you can trust. Each one is beautifully illustrated with a sequence of drawings.

Tides & Currents by David Arnold. Explains how to predict what the tide will do over the racecourse, then use the flow to win.

Race Training by Rick White. Drills to make you a champion.

Winning in One Designs by Dave Perry. The classic book on every aspect of racing.

FOR YOUR YOUNGER BROTHER OR SISTER

Sailing for Kids by Gary & Steve Kibble. Explains how to sail the Optimist. This is the official handbook for the RYA Young Opportunity Scheme.

Racing: A Beginner's Manual by Tim Davison & John Caig. Explains how to get started in racing.

The Racing Rules Companion by Bryan Wills. Flip cards (in full colour) give the key rules.